Music of the Sea

RULE BRITANNIA,

NATIONAL SONG AND CHORUS,

NEWLY ARRANGED EXPRESSLY FOR THIS WORK.

ENT. STAT. HALL.   THE MUSICAL TREASURY.   PRICE THREEPENCE.

PUBLISHED AT PETER'S HILL, NEAR ST. PAUL'S.

55

Music of the Sea

David Proctor

Edited by Richard Baker OBE, RD

Critical acclaim for recent NMMP books:

Treasures of the National Maritime Museum
Edited by Gloria Clifton and Nigel Rigby

'The book is fabulous, the collection well represented and broad. Here you will find not only the great sea battles, but also pictures of migrants forced overseas by poverty, the sailor's story as well as the admiral's.'
MAGGIE MCDONALD, NEW SCIENTIST

'Britain should be thankful to the National Maritime Museum, which is in effect the museum of British history, and a phenomenal reservoir of material document-ing the growth of a once great maritime power ... The pictures are the point, but the book is also enhanced with brief but useful essays, on the discovery of latitude and longitude, for example; on the voyages for slaves, spices and settlement, and on the great transatlantic crossings ... This book is a taste ... of what [those who have never visited the museum] have been missing.'
TIM RADFORD, THE GUARDIAN

'The title *Treasures* is correct: each item inside has been so well photographed, so exceptionally reproduced, that they leap off the page ... This is a beautiful, grace-ful book and its editors ... should be proud.'
ED EWING, THE GUIDE

Nelson's Fleet at Trafalgar
Brian Lavery

'A new study of the campaign, told in a unique and vivid style ... This should be an essential addition to any library on Trafalgar, and will be in the vanguard of the many books published to commemorate the bicentenary.'
PAUL CHAMBERLAIN, FIRST EMPIRE

'Within its covers is skilfully compressed an immense subject and it deserves wide success.'
RICHARD WOODMAN, MARITIME LIFE AND TRADITIONS

'Naval book readers need to keep their nerve as Nelson and Trafalgar books roll off the presses in the run up to the battle's bicentenary ... but the bold will grasp this attractive new title issued by the National Maritime Museum and written by their distinguished Curator of Naval History ... The reader ... needs a guide and in Brian Lavery he has the best.'
LAWRENCE PHILLIPS, SHIPS TELEGRAPH

The Captain's Table
Sarah Edington

'[An] elegant book … Apart from the atmospheric photographs and illustrations, the great joy of this book are the 70 or so classic recipes, all of them taken from original menus and adapted for a modern audience.'
YOU, THE MAIL ON SUNDAY

'Those golden years of carefree cruising are captured … As well as evoking the style and opulence of those days, the book includes … many dishes served up by leading chefs.'
PAUL CALLAN, THE SUNDAY EXPRESS

Hostilities Only: Training the Wartime Royal Navy
Brian Lavery

'… the first comprehensive history of how this first real citizens' navy was recruited, organised and prepared for active duty … The personal memories of Hostilities Only sailors enliven this fine work by one of Britain's leading naval historians.'
LAWRENCE PHILLIPS, SHIPS TELEGRAPH

'Mr Lavery's style is terse and to-the-point and his facts are well marshalled; *Hostilities Only* is a fine exposition on the underbelly of naval history … Highly recommended for serious students of life at sea.'
RICHARD WOODMAN, NUMAST TELEGRAPH

Animals at Sea
Liza Verity

'… a haunting insight into the lives of men and animals in a bygone age … This is a book which celebrates the relationship between man and animal … Just right for auntie or uncle's Christmas stocking!'
LOUISE WARBURTON, PARROTS

'… capture[s] the almost tangible bond between animal and owner. The pictures often show the animals being showered with attention by the lonely sailors or reclining on the deck in splendour … All in all, an entertaining afternoon's read and a treasure for pet lovers …'
NAMRATA NADKARNI, LLOYD'S LIST

www.nmm.ac.uk/publishing

First Published in 2005 by
National Maritime Publishing
Greenwich, London, SE10 9NF

www.nmm.ac.uk/publishing

ISBN 0948065613

1 2 3 4 5 6 7 8 9

A CIP catalogue record for this book is available from the
British Library.

Project managed by Eleanor Dryden
Editorial, design and production by The Book Group

Printed and bound in China on behalf of Compass Press Ltd.

HALF-TITLE *Concertina, c. 1860.*

FRONTISPIECE *'Rule Britannia'. Its sentiments may be outdated, but it still
stirs the heart of a maritime nation.*

Contents

Bass drum from the battle-cruiser HMS Lion, *the flagship of Vice-Admiral Sir David Beatty at three major engagements of the First World War.*

Foreword

'Music', declared the Chinese philosopher Confucius some two-and-a-half thousand years ago, 'produces a kind of pleasure which human nature cannot do without'; and as the late David Proctor makes clear in the pages which follow, music has proved just as indispensable at sea as on land. Many studies have been published on different aspects of sea–music, but when this volume first appeared in 1992 it was a pioneering survey of the subject as a whole, and so far as I know remains unique in its field.

I have been asked to update David Proctor's work in a few minor respects, and I am very happy to be associated with it, as one who has experienced music at sea in various forms in the course of a long life.

When I joined the navy as an Ordinary Seaman in 1943, I found that one of my messmates on the lower deck of a minesweeper played the French horn, which by hard-won consent he was allowed to practice for a brief period each day. Thus I became acquainted for the first time with the horn calls from Wagner's *Siegfried* and with the amazing tolerance of the British sailor. Later, as a Midshipman, I was appointed to a sloop serving in the Battle of the Atlantic, and the Captain, hearing that I played the piano, insisted on installing a small yacht-piano in the officers' Wardroom. On it I was expected to play not Mozart sonatas but a selection of bawdy nautical ditties, and thus I acquired a useful new repertoire. In more recent times I have visited a number of Royal Navy ships and found that music is still much in evidence. One guided-missile destroyer had a respectable amateur band and an Electronic Warfare Officer who played the concert harp, a rather large object to deal with in a crowded warship. 'Where do you practice?' I asked him. 'In the Officers' Heads (toilets)', he replied; 'The seat is just the right height and the acoustics are marvellous'.

For the last two decades I have been closely involved with music afloat in much larger ships as the host of P&O's Music Festivals at Sea, building on the long tradition of musical entertainment in deep-sea passenger vessels. For many years I was regularly reminded of the appeal of sea music at the Royal Albert Hall, as a TV presenter at the Last Night of the Proms, and as compere of the Mountbatten Festival of Music presented annually by the band service of the Royal Marines.

This revised edition of *Music of the Sea* has been produced under the auspices of the National Maritime Museum, Greenwich, which has many relevant musical artefacts and documents in its collections, and I should like to express my thanks for the help I have received from Rachel Giles, the Museum's Head of Publishing, and other members of the Museum's staff. David Proctor's thanks are expressed overleaf.

Richard Baker, OBE, RD

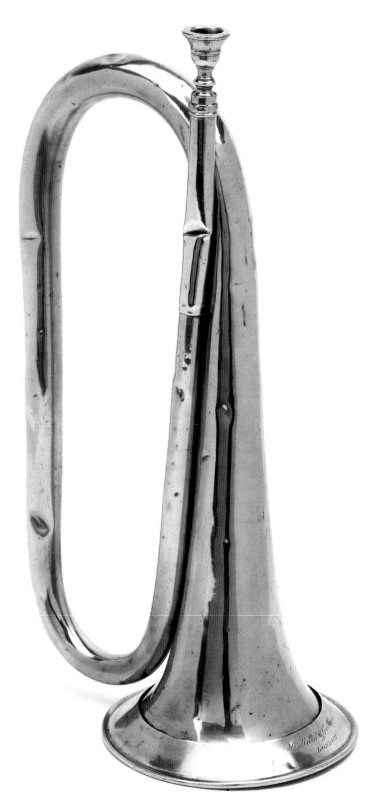

Bugle used by naval brigades serving in the Crimea and during the Indian Mutiny, formerly in the possession of Capt. Sir William Peel KCB, VC (1824–58).

Author's Acknowledgements

I am most grateful for the widespread and generous support I have received during the preparation of this book. I only hope that in the following list of individuals and organisations I have included all those who principally deserve my thanks.

Firstly, I am most appreciative of the financial grant awarded by the Caird Fund Committee of the National Maritime Museum, which enabled me to travel far more widely than would otherwise have been possible. I am also truly grateful to the main Trustees of the Museum and to my colleagues there.

I have received particularly significant help from Surgeon Vice-Admiral Sir James Watt, and from Oliver Davies of the Royal College of Music, where the Library staff have given unstinting assistance. Valuable help also came from the Music Library at the British Library and from colleagues in other British maritime museums. Colleagues from the International Commission for Maritime History and the British Commission have been very encouraging. Lieutenant-Colonel John Ware, former Principal Director of Music, Royal Marines, John Trendell who has written the history of the RM bands, and Mr Colin Bowden, have been more than generous of their time; so has Dr John De Courcy Ireland of the Irish Maritime History Institute.

I have also received much impressive encouragement and advice from other countries. In France, from the Musée de la Marine and the Archives Nationales in Paris, and the Service Historique de la Marine at Vincennes; in Germany from the Deutsches Schiffahrtsmuseum, from the Stadtmuseum, Dusseldorf and the Stadtmuseum, Munich. In Belgium, I am indebted to the Nationaal Scheepvaart Museum in Antwerp, and in the Netherlands to the University of Leiden, the Nederlands Scheepvaart Museum of Amsterdam, the Prins Hendrik Maritiem Museum of Rotterdam, the Haags Gemeentemuseum, and the Rijksarchief at Middelburg in Zeeland. In Norway I was helped by the Sjøfartsmuseum, Oslo, and by the Bergen Sjøfartsmuseum; in Denmark by the Handel-og Söfartsmuseet at Elsinore; while in Sweden, Skans and Vicky Torsten Nilsson were particularly supportive.

Further south, I received a great welcome and much help in Spain from Dr Julian de Zulueta, and the staffs of the Museo Naval and the Instituto de Historia y Cultura Naval in Madrid, while in Portugal I have reason to thank the Museu de Marinha in Lisbon and officers of the Portuguese naval band service. In Italy I had much helpful advice from Professor Luigi da Rosa and Professor Ugo Tucci.

I was assisted by many colleagues in the USA, especially Stuart Frank and Mary Molloy of the Kendall Whaling Museum, whose work on shanties and sea songs is outstanding.

Most of all, I am grateful to my wife and family without whose patience, practical help and understanding, this book would not have been possible.

Musical boxes were useful ready-made purveyors of music afloat. This one, c. 1750, with Greenwich Hospital portrayed on the lid, was made by the Swiss firm of E Paillard.

Introduction

We all need certain comforts and supports as we make our way through life. Some, such as a roof over our heads, a warm fire, the company of friends and the love of a family, we are inclined to take for granted; others we have to reach out for.

What about music? In an age when we are almost overwhelmed by music – transmitted by radio and television, reproduced on CDs, videos and DVDs – few would deny that music in some form either inspires, entertains or comforts the mind. There are even those who cannot take a walk or ride a bicycle without the aid of a personal stereo and earphones pounding away. Car drivers tear about in a metal cocoon, its sides quivering with blasted sound. It was not always so.

Until about 200 years ago music was generally only available to those who attended church, who heard street musicians in a town, or listened to the bawdy folk music of the tavern. Of course, there were those who amused themselves with playing their own, sometimes very crude, instruments, but they were always in the minority. As for the opportunity to learn to play a fine instrument alone or in concert with others, this was granted only to those from well-established families and those who were educated in a great religious institution, or attended a noble or royal court. Music in some form was, therefore, available to many, but the effective transmission of music to the masses awaited the creation of concert halls in the late seventeenth century, and the later invention of gramophones, radio and modern technological aids.

What then, I have often wondered, was the position of the professional seaman and of those who travelled by sea? Living in often very uncomfortable and, often frightening surroundings, assaulted by the elemental forces of the sea and weather, did they give up all hope of hearing or playing any music? Did they simply abandon their spirits to a soggy acceptance of their fate? For us today, the thought of taking passage in a wooden-built sailing vessel, poorly lit, smelly, damp, fitted with very cramped accommodation, and dependent on favourable winds for a safe and speedy passage, is soothingly remote. Yet such an environment was commonplace just over a 150 years ago. Conditions on land were not necessarily much better, as we see in the world that Charles Dickens described so vividly. Because we would find such conditions quite revolting, we should not be misled into imagining the people who lived in them felt the same. It was their world, and they were used to it. At least some sort of food was provided regularly, and crude accommodation was available, to counterbalance the risk of drowning.

But what of food for the mind and spirit? Did the seafarer, whether professional or passenger, have any particular needs that were different from the landsman? What sort of music was available and what instruments were used to play it? When was it played and by whom?

These are fascinating questions, but difficult to answer fully for, except in the cases of official naval bands and of music provided in late nineteenth- and twentieth-century merchant ships owned and managed by large public companies, few records exist. Hence a search through many sources: personal papers, printed reports and manuscript journals, was needed in order to find snippets of knowledge that might be woven into an acceptable pattern.

A Universal Currency

It is an intriguing pattern, crossing the boundaries of the social history of sea-farers and of the history of music; and it cannot be narrowed down to the characteristics of seafarers from one particular nation. By the very nature of their work sailors are forever travelling from one country to another, trans-porting passengers and cargo, influencing each other in a swirl of interna-tional cross currents. A melody that originated in one country would be swiftly learnt, adapted and given words from another. This was, and still is, a truly multinational culture, a hotchpotch bred of the people and the condi-tions in which they travelled and worked.

It is clear that the seafarer has always had just as great a need of music as the landsman, and has done his best to perform and enjoy it. Much of the music would have been in the broad category of folk music, but the patterns of development roughly followed those found ashore. The performance of concert music at sea awaited the advent of larger passenger vessels that could provide the comfortable conditions required.

Three main kinds of sea music can be discerned. Firstly, the music played for morale boosting and for ceremonial or diplomatic reasons, which, general-ly speaking, originated with trumpeters and drummers and developed into the official maintenance of naval or marine bands; secondly, the casual, informal music played principally for entertainment and for dancing, which could be a most important form of exercise in the confined space of a sailing ship; and thirdly, the shanty, working music and the sea song. Each type has its own char-acter and its own story, but their origins are interwoven and share the all important artistic and therapeutic functions of music. These may be the finest expressions of emotion, the maintenance of morale or sheer entertainment. All serve a common cause: the nourishment of good spirits amongst a group of people who are literally 'all in the same boat.'

Sounds and Superstition

Underlying this need for music are aspects of the beliefs, the superstitions, the spiritual world of the professional seaman, which, in some degree, is trans-mitted to the passenger. Here the seaman of the past and to some extent today, is different from the landsman. Faced with the continuing demand to make the best of tides, currents and weather, in the freezing, gale-strewn win-ter, in fair trade winds or the heat of the doldrums, the old sailing ship sea-man had a special affinity with his natural environment and a particular sen-sitivity to it. Especially in the early period there was a respect for the ele-mental forces of the sea and an acute awareness of threatening dangers. It was as well not to irritate these by playing the wrong music at the wrong moment. To whistle or play loudly during a calm might bring more wind than was welcome. Sounds that jarred could cause trouble wider than mere annoyance to shipmates and fellow passengers. There was also the matter of pleasing the spiritual character of the ship, with which she was endowed when the shipbuilder created her from the living organism of timber and which was fêted at her launch.

There is a fourth category of sea music, which is not designed for performance in ships, but is inspired by the sea and by those who face its dangers. This category ranges from major works produced by some of the world's greatest composers to ballads and other slighter pieces, many of them destined for use around the parlour piano of bygone days. Sea music of this kind is still capable of moving and exciting us, witness the continuing appeal of Henry Wood's 'Sea Songs' fantasia at the Last Night of the Proms. Great sea events, such as the loss of the *Titanic* and Nelson's death at the moment of victory in the Battle of Trafalgar, inspired reams of musical offerings, most of them strong in sentiment but feeble in musical quality.

Such a broad canvas might seem confusing, but I have found a unifying strand in it, the need that men and women in any situation have for music. This absolute desire is in us all. I have tried to discover how this was met in what were and are very special circumstances: the heaving, salty, damp world of the sea, which many of us would consider quite unsympathetic to playing or to composing music.

Violin played by Rear-Admiral Sir W E Parry on his Arctic Expedition (1819–27).

1 Music Takes to the Water

Music can be made anywhere, is invisible and does not smell.

W H Auden

Perhaps the earliest recorded waterborne professional musician is the player of a clarinet-like instrument depicted in the bows of a boat in the tomb of Seshemnefer at Giza in Egypt and dated about 2450 BC. The instrument might be a trumpet-like speaking tube, but is more likely to be a reed instrument. Of a slightly later date are the unnamed harpist and singer who performed for the Egyptian Meket-Re on the River Nile, *c.* 2000 BC. The scene is depicted in a model discovered in the XIth Dynasty tomb of Meket-Re and now in the Metropolitan Museum of New York, and is described thus: 'On one boat the owner, Meket-Re, sits before his cabin, receiving a report from the captain of the vessel and listening to a blind harp-er and a singer, who pats his mouth with his hand to give his voice a war-bling sound'. The harpist's instrument has 'a small sound-box decorated on the upper side with a pattern imitating an animal's skin. The nine suspension pegs are of alternating colours'.[1]

With one celebrated exception, records of ancient Egyptian water-borne musicians are scant. There is a note by Herodotus of men and women singing and playing clappers and a form of double oboe, while on their way by boat to an annual festival in honour of the cat goddess Baster, who had a shrine in the Delta at Bastasis, but this is of a fairly late date (*c.* 450 BC). There are one or two examples of a form of working song, especially amongst fisher-men hauling in their nets. Music to help with rhythmic work such as that of oarsmen, was practiced, for example on the important occasion recorded by the historian Plutarch when Cleopatra was rowed out to meet Mark Antony. Shakespeare, using Plutarch as his guide, expresses it thus:

> … the oars were silver,
> Which to the tune of flutes kept stroke, and made
> The water which they beat to follow faster,
> As amorous of their strokes.
>
> *Antony and Cleopatra, II ii.*

Shakespeare's 'flutes' were more likely the double pipes, or pan pipes intro-duced in Ptolemaic times, probably from Greece where they occur about 400 BC.

The Greek oarsmen, of roughly the same period, who sweated at the heavy oars in their great triremes and other galleys may have had wind instruments to accompany them, but their musical tradition was more vocal in character. The evidence indicates that the oarsmen repeated a kind of chant, which both occupied their minds and helped maintain the rhythm of rowing. The chant could be altered to meet the needs for different speeds – for cruising or for ramming in battle. The powerful, dominant beat of a drum was not needed, because the rowers were highly prized athletic freemen, who did not require this kind of discipline, as did slaves in the later war-galleys of other nations. Interestingly, the use of a chant was practiced to very good effect in the recent reconstruction of a Greek trireme rowed in Greek waters by a mixed crew of amateurs.[2]

Early Music of the North

In northern Europe a different form of documentary evidence for professional musicians of a similar period to the blind Egyptian harper has been found in the Bronze Age rock carvings or engravings of southern Sweden and the Norway border area.[3] These frequently showed people in ships taking part in seasonal festivities, or ceremonials in honour of ships, the sea, and of fishing. In one scene dancing is taking place and accompanying the dancers are musicians playing lyres – tall horn-like instruments made of bronze with something of the appearance of a straightened sousaphone. In other scenes more formal activities are taking place.[4] Played by a skilled musician the lyre can produce a range of soft sounds from its fundamental note to eleven harmonics above, which would have been apt for ceremonies and festivities.

Many examples have been found, often in pairs, and have been preserved in institutions such as the Danish National Museum in Copenhagen.

Other instruments have been found in Viking ship-burial sites, such as the whistle found in the ninth-century Gokstad ship, now preserved in the Viking Ship Museum in Oslo. Similarly, a lyre was found in the Sutton Hoo ship-burial find near Woodbridge in England. Probably this was the site of the burial of a very important East Anglian king of the seventh century, King Raedwald, who died in AD 624–5. A pipe was found very recently in a shipyard site on the Danish island of Falster. Dated 1080, this pipe is the oldest known wind instrument fitted with a reed that has been found in Scandinavia and may well have been played afloat.[5]

For the Viking people living in small coastal or fjord-side communities, set between high mountains, boats were vital to everyday life, as the only practicable form of transport and communication. Food, people, animals, metal ores were all carried by water. Strongly built sea and even ocean-going ships were used to launch raids on other countries and to establish settlements overseas, thus extending Viking dominions. With this emphasis on ships and boats it is not surprising to find that in addition to its practical value as a means of transport, the ship was revered as the bearer of Life. In Viking cult rites the sun, the giver of life, was borne by day in a horse-drawn chariot or on horseback, but at night it was borne in a ship. Since in cold winter months the night-time was protracted, the role of the ship in bearing the life-giving sun safely was most important. Probably this symbolism was extended to embrace the idea of the ship actually preserving life in the dread days of winter and then bringing it back in the welcome days of spring. Regrettably there was no means then of recording the movement of the dancers and the music in these rituals. Nevertheless, we obtain some idea from the lyres and from other instruments that have been found, like the ninth-century bone flutes excavated at Viking sites such as Haithabu and Birka, which could play a range of about five harmonics.

The story of the achievements and culture of these people is told in part at least in the Sagas, the great free-verse Nordic epic accounts of voyages, battles, kings and of myths. Some were never written down and have been lost, but others have survived. Recent research has shown that from about AD 650, rowing officers or 'skalds' were carried in Viking ships to lead a working chant for the oarsmen, who formed the all-important engine room of the ship and whose services might be desperately needed to escape from the hot pursuit of an enemy or to reach a destination before all aboard perished. The single sail carried in the ship might not serve if the winds were contrary. The chants had a rhythm that allowed the oarsmen to count the number of strokes they rowed in units of eight, the number of fingers appearing on the upper part of the oar as a man gripped it. In turn this could be used to indicate the time that a man should row before being relieved. It also seems likely that the units were used to calculate roughly the distance covered by the ship in the time period involved.

The character of the chants was not entirely functional. They included epic lyrical sections, which told of the achievements of the ship and praised the bravery and skill of her captain, who was possibly the leader of a whole expedition, and from whom the rowers hoped to receive a good reward for their hard work at sea and for their bravery in battle.[6]

Waterborne Minstrels

To some degree the chants resemble the character of the sagas and of the songs of the early medieval European gleemen, harpists or courtiers who entertained their royal or noble masters at a feast or whilst on a journey. There are early references in German literature to such musicians performing during voyages on inland waterways. Thus in the poem 'Mosella' of AD 370 by the Roman tutor Ausonius the barge skipper sings a humorous song whilst sailing on the Mosel. In AD 588 Venantius Fortunatus from Ravenna wrote of a journey, also on the Mosel, which he undertook whilst in the service of King Childebert II. During the journey the retinue entertained themselves by singing, accompanied by a recorder and a stringed instrument, probably a harp.

Harpists served in every country of Europe and they travelled widely, sometimes in a retinue and sometimes alone, for the profession of minstrels was well accepted and respected in the early medieval period. In Germany they included such outstanding musicians as the thirteenth-century Walter von der Vogelweide and his slightly later, half-legendary contemporary, Tannhäuser.[7] The minstrel Taillefer is supposed to have accompanied the Norman Duke William on his invasion of England and probably played during the Channel crossing to maintain the spirits of the soldiers crouching in their ships. He was killed early on in the Battle of Hastings, after making himself an obvious target by playing vigorously before the Norman soldiers, in order to encourage them to fight well. The Normans, of Viking stock and with the same restless character, spread their culture and their music, as well as their administrative and military heritage, as far as Sicily and the Mediterranean.

The music that the minstrels played at sea would have varied little from what they played on land, and would have owed much to the music of the contemporary Christian Church, which was the prime vehicle for the spread of musical knowledge in Europe. Music was and still is an important ornament to the Mass, and whenever missionaries such as St Augustine, who came to Kent in England in AD 597, travelled and practiced their faith, they also brought their skills in music, using these as an aid to acceptance of that faith.

Ordinary seamen would undoubtedly have heard some of this music and might have joined in parts of the Masses, but these were sung in Latin, which would have made it difficult for them. However, professional musicians were able to adapt church music to the composition of popular songs more suited to the seamen's taste. That this occurred into the seventeenth century is well established.

In the archives of the great trading city of Bruges, there are fascinating references to English sailor minstrels of 1344 serving under Edward III, who was campaigning in Flanders. Florentine ships' minstrels of sixty years later were also mentioned. In 1447–8 a Venetian trumpeter named Zorzi Trombetta, who travelled in a galley and who played on demand at weddings and festivities, visited Sandwich in Kent and Sluys, the outport of Bruges. His manuscript collection of music is preserved in the British Library.[8]

Sea Music and the Crusaders

The leader of the Christian Church in 1095, Pope Urban II, was responsible for initiating the Crusades, the great campaigns originally undertaken for the protection of Christian pilgrims to the Holy Land. Many European monarchs took part, and great armies were transported across the Mediterranean. The Crusades, which extended over a period of 200 years, brought about a great deal of seaborne movement of people from West to East and back. Consequently, it was also one of the most significant moments for the transmission and absorption of different cultures, including music.

Kings and nobles who wished to maintain their standing took their professional musicians with them, in order to announce their arrival, welcome guests, and bid farewell with proper ceremony and celebration. So we find in a manuscript at the Bibliothèque Nationale in Paris an illustration of the disembarkation of King Louis IX of France at Damietta in 1249. In this we observe that trumpeters are playing in the aftercastle of the ship, announcing the royal arrival.

Drums and trumpets are also mentioned as being played at the arrival of another crusading monarch, the English king, Richard I (1157-99), in Sicily. It is said he came, 'with many buccas and other large vessels and galleys, in such pomp and splendour, that the resounding trumpets and loud horns struck fear and dread into the souls of the citizens'.[9]

In 1202 the fleet for the Fourth Crusade was led on its departure from Venice by the Doge, Enrico Dandolo, in person, aboard his splendid galley, in the bows of which, 'there blew four silver horns [trumpets] and cymbals played in a festive manner'. In the various ships there were, 'good 100 couple of horns, some of silver, others of copper, which all sounded at the sailing, and so many cymbals, drums and other instruments that it was quite wonderful'.[10] We know that the musicians in any official Venetian ships were professionally employed, because the Statutes of the City, dated 1172, laid down that vessels of lesser tonnage would carry two trumpets; those of heavier tonnage one trumpet, a drum and two kettledrums.

Other professional musicians carried in royal ships included troubadours and trouvères, who had largely replaced minstrels in European courts and who were of a higher order socially and professionally. The troubadours were both musicians and poets, who originated from southern France, the provinces of Languedoc and Provence especially, and from Italy. They were usually, but not always, children of nobility and were given the finest patronage and support, thriving in courts where their abilities were appreciated and prized. Richard I of England was himself a troubadour. He was strongly influenced by his mother, Eleanor of Aquitaine, whose family had been great patrons of troubadours, and by links which both he and his father, Henry II, had with their French dominions. He attracted the finest troubadours to his court, amongst them Arnaut Daniel and Bertran de Born as well as the trouvère Blondel de Nesle. The latter is supposed to have assisted with the rescue of Richard, who had been captured on his return from the crusades and imprisoned by Leopold of Austria, by playing a song known to them both, at various castles until he heard his master respond. The trouvères came from northern and central France and used a different dialect from that of the troubadours.

The words of many troubadour and trouvère poems have survived, but far fewer melodies. Amongst the latter is one of Portuguese origin that is typical of their character, expressing the lyrical romantic qualities of life, 'Romance da Dona Infanta'. The setting of the story in the crusades makes it quite topical, and it may well have been played en route to the Holy Land.[11]

A different survival is one of the songs of Walter von der Vogelweide, who accompanied the Emperor Frederick II on the Sixth Crusade (1228-9), and who probably saw him crowned King of Jerusalem in 1229. During the Crusade Walter composed his well-known 'Palestine Song', which has survived with its music. The words have a devout character and are set to what is almost a Gregorian chant. They perhaps reflect Walter's gratitude for survival after a demanding voyage. Another German song of the same period that has survived with its music is also a crusader's song. It, too, has a firm religious character but there is no knowledge of the author. This is 'In Gotts Namen fahren wir' (We travel in the name of God).[12]

The Sound of Bells

From their crusading contact with the Middle East, Europeans gained knowledge of a whole range of percussion instruments: cymbals, tambourine, triangle and the naqqara or small kettledrum, which was

usually mounted in pairs. Knowledge of the cymbala or peal of small bells, which was played with a little hammer, had spread earlier via Byzantium and the Christian Church. This was an attractive instrument, which evolved into the carillon that is often to be found in churches in the Low Countries especially, augmenting the peal of big bells. These instruments were all principally made of metal – copper, brass or bronze – and were typical of Arabian skills in this field. It's interesting to note that a full carillon of bells was installed on board a replica built in 1990 of a Russian Pomor koch. This type of vessel was originally used in the

The ship's bell from the Mary Rose, *cast in 1510 in Flanders. Is this the oldest surviving English ship's bell?*

fifteenth and sixteenth centuries for trading around the North Cape and into the Baltic. It has to be said there is some doubt whether the koches of old carried carillons: the builder of the replica, it seems, wanted to turn his whole ship into a musical instrument, rightly thinking that the sound of bells would carry well across quiet waters and enhance interest in his enterprise.[13]

Did crusading contacts influence the use of bells on board British and other ships to mark the passage of time? The answer is uncertain, but it is known that bells were used in this way from the thirteenth century onwards. They were struck every half-hour, taking their time from the passage of sand through a 'half-hour glass'. Rather like an egg-timer, it had to be reversed when all the sand had run through, thus providing a cue for the bell-striker. For centuries

Ship ready for battle, manned by armed soldiers and trumpeters. Luttrell Psalter, c. 1320.

the ship's bell was also used to announce the vessel's presence in poor visibility. Under those conditions it would be rung for five seconds every minute.

A Flourish of Trumpets

The musicians most frequently described in documents and shown in depictions of shipboard life from the early medieval period to the late seventeenth century are trumpeters. They are seen in manuscript miniatures, early mural paintings, carvings, official seals of ports such as Winchelsea, Rouen and Yarmouth of the late twelfth century, and later in drawings, engravings, grisailles and oil paintings.

In battle a trumpeter's life could be very dangerous. There is a vivid picture of this in a description of the Battle of Zierikzee fought in 1304:

> Pedrogue, whose ship had drifted off with the incoming tide, profits from the disorder to attack L'Orgueilleuse of Bruges. With the two short range heavy crossbows, which he has on board his flagship, he pours a hail of heavy bolts against his adversary; one of the surges of bolts flies through the galleries of the forecastle where the trumpeters are sounding their silver trumpets; and such is the force of the shot that one of the musicians has his arm torn off, a second his stomach shot through and the entrails as light as air are spread all over the palisade of the after castle.
>
> *[Author's translation]*

The chronicler Guiart records that in Pedrogue's own ships trumpets sounded, drums rolled and pipers played to encourage his men.[14]

Laurence Minot writing in 1352 of events in the reign of Edward III describes the Battle of Sluys (1340) when Edward's fleet defeated the Normans. He mentions:

> John of Aile of the Sluys with scheltron ful schene
> Was comen into Cagent, cantly and kene,
> Bot sone was his trumping turned to tene;
> Of him had Sir Edward his will als I wene.

(With great eagerness Jan van Fyle and his squadron all shining came from Sluys to Cadzant, but their trumpeting was soon turned to notes of sadness; King Edward defeated him, as I know.)

The same author, writing of the Battle of Les Espagnols Sur Mer, which took place at Winchelsea in 1350, describes King Edward's fleet:

> Thai sailed furth in the Swin in a somers tyde,
> With trompes and taburns and mekill other pride.[15]

(They sailed forth from the Swin in a summer's tide, with trumpets, tabors and much other pride.)

The first mention of the trumpet is lost in the mists of time, but the Egyptians and the Romans used it, mainly for military signalling purposes and this was its most important role both on land and at sea.[16] For this reason its use was strictly regulated and was reserved for people of the highest rank, either in person or by their official heralds and musicians. In 1528 an Imperial Decree was promulgated by Charles V, laying down the conditions for the use of the trumpet. This was extended to kettledrums by the establishment of the Imperial Guild of Court and Field Trumpeters and Court Army Kettledrummers in 1623. The kettledrums concerned are the larger type that we see today and which replaced the small, paired type or naqqara.[17]

In England, use of the trumpet was reserved for monarchs and those they wished to patronise with their royal favour or who were appointed as high officers of state, including admirals. Supervision of trumpeters gradually delegated to the King's Musick, a group of royal musicians paid from the Privy Purse by the Lord Chamberlain. From the sixteenth century the officers in charge had the ranks of Master of the King's Musick and Sergeant Trumpeter. The Master had overall control, stemming from the group of musicians and choristers based on the Chapel Royal, but the Sergeant Trumpeter had considerable power over the public use of trumpets in particular and could charge fees or impose penalties for improper use. Subject to royal command he could appoint the trumpeters to serve at sea. For example Charles Howard, Lord Effingham and Earl of Nottingham, 1536–1624, was appointed Lord High Admiral in 1585, and, as befitted his rank and station, trumpeters from the Queen's Musick were nominated to attend upon him. They were Stephen Medcalf, Richard Frynde, Thomas Westcrosse and Peter Farewell, and they were provided with white and green cloth, Tudor colours 'for cassocks and Maryners sloppes'. In 1579 a warrant was issued for sea liveries for William Lyndsey and Thomas Holdsworth, 'trumpettours' appointed to serve on the seas under Admiral Sir John Parrot. These appointments and liveries were renewed in 1580 at Michaelmas. They are among the earliest records of the official appointment of musicians to serve at sea in the English fleet and of dress for them.[18]

Charles Howard was Commander-in-Chief of the English fleet that fought the Spanish Armada in 1588. The opposing Spanish fleet included official galleons and galleasses in which the normal maximum number of trumpeters carried was six. For battle two drummers and a fife player were added, probably with soldiers embarked to reinforce the number of men capable of hand-to-hand fighting. Their orders for battle were to play incessantly with the greatest bravura to enliven their own companions and to frighten the enemy. Thus one has a marvellous mental picture of the opposing musicians hurling defiance at each other across the waters of the English channel.[19]

2 Sounds of Supremacy at Sea

Sound the trumpets, beat the drums!

John Dryden, Alexander's Feast

Music and the Early Explorers

Following periods of strife on the home front, such as the Wars of the Roses (1455–85) in England, and the fight against the occupying Moorish power in Spain, in which warring factions struggled to gain dominion over their own national affairs, European nations turned their attention to the wider campaign necessary to improve their commercial, and financial strength. It had been perceived that direct trading by sea in home-administered ships was the solution to creating expansion of trade. This required significant national investment in voyages of exploration to discover and record routes to the Far East and to the then scarcely known North and South American continents. Monarchs summoned up their financial resources and borrowed money from South German bankers to launch experienced and trained sea captains, accompanied by managing nobility, military officers and men in available ships of appropriate size and strength to make transoceanic voyages in search of trading wealth or gold.

The first nation to undertake the organisation of these extensive maritime enterprises, the equivalent in terms of the available technology of space probes today, was Portugal, after Prince Henry 'the Navigator' had the experience of meeting North African trading merchants at the time of the siege of Ceuta in 1415. It was natural that trumpeters and drummers should be included in the manning of official ships, and so they were. How far the royal authorities realised that musicians would have a significant role is unknown, but music proved to be of great importance for maintaining morale amongst the crew and as an essential form of non-verbal communication between two peoples who could not understand each other's languages. Music was neutral in character and encouraged an atmosphere of mutual confidence and understanding in what might otherwise be an antagonistic situation. Additionally, music was used for entertainment, and to provide working rhythms on long, ardous voyages in uncharted seas and demanding climatic conditions.

Alvaro Velho records the cardinal moment in Vasco da Gama's epic voyage to India, when on 20 November 1497 the battered ships and crews finally rounded the Cape of Good Hope:

> On Saturday we saw the Cape of Good Hope but had a contrary wind from the SSE and the Cape bore SE–NE. So we turned to seaward and went away from the coast and on 20 November when we were going along the coast to the east the wind came from the stern, so that we rejoiced with dancing and playing the

trumpets and drums throughout the fleet because our trust in
the bounty of the Lord had been fulfilled.[20]

[Author's translation]

Shortly after this exhausting and tricky rounding of the Cape, Vasco da Gama
opened negotiations with the natives of the east coast of Africa near the point
where Bartholomew Diaz had put ashore ten years earlier. The same author
records, after drawing attention to their arrival by firing guns and having an
initial meeting with some natives that:

On Saturday came more than twelve negroes, men and boys
with twelve cattle and four sheep. And when we went on land
they began to play four flutes in four voices [parts] which is
usual among the natives. And when he heard this, Vasco da
Gama ordered the trumpets to play and we danced.

[Author's translation][21]

On his voyage to India ten years later we are told how another Portuguese
captain, Lopo Soarez, took some portable organs with him as gifts:

He took two pages dressed in livery and six trumpets with flags
of silk and he took some portative organs, which he had in a box
in his ship and gave them to the King of Cananor as a present.

[Author's translation]

Later:

When Lopo Soarez came on board the ship he ordered all the
artillery to fire and all the trumpets and drums to play, and our
organs began to play and there came from the shore a great
multitude of Moors and Gentiles who were afraid.[22]

[Author's translation]

Whilst the prime motivation for the voyages of discovery was commercial, they
had another underlying purpose, which was significant in terms of obtaining
approval from the powerful spiritual authorities of the day and thereby further
support from crowned heads and the highest echelons of the nobility, especially in Spain and Portugal where the Roman Catholic Church was very influential. This was the missionary purpose of converting the native peoples to
Christianity, which helped to assuage European Christian consciences for the
failure of the crusades and gave another opportunity to dent the power of the
infidel by taking the hearts of his people as well as his trade and wealth.

In this context Christopher Columbus is a most important figure for
although he could scarcely be classed as a religious missionary, he had a deep
and abiding personal faith that helped him overcome great difficulties, to his
dying moment. It was the music of this faith that Columbus took with him on
his great voyage of 1492. Whilst he had no official drummers and trumpeters,
he did have choir boys whose task it was to sing the chants at the break of day:

> Blessed by the light of day
> And the Holy Cross we say ...

And at the turn of the half-hour glass, a chant such as:

> Five is past and six floweth
> More shall flow if God willeth,
> Count and pass make voyage fast;

and at sunset:

> God give us a good night and good sailing
> May our ship make a good passage
> Sir Captain and Master and good company.

The 'Salve Regina' was then sung to a Benedictine chant.[23]

Mass was sung regularly unless foul weather prevented this, and whilst the seamen's idea of singing was pretty crude and its musical quality highly debatable, the chants and the mass were an essential element of their daily life.

The religious, missionary element remained an important feature of the later Spanish voyages and exploring enterprises. Along with the harsh battle-forged soldiers of fortune and the conquistadores went the Franciscan friars and priests convinced of the need to spread their faith to the natives. Strange fellow travellers were these, the scholarly brothers who recorded so much of North and South American culture to our great benefit, and the harsh, graspingly ambitious military men whose manic lust for gold and power led them to commit fearful atrocities, fight each other and deceive the innocent. Both shared the liturgical music of their faith and whilst this had some value for the soldiers, it was of much greater value to the missionary friars who were the true professional musicians of the voyages, and who made use of their music after their arrival to help communication with the natives and their conversion to the Christian faith. The friars found a very rich native musical tradition, especially in Mexico, Peru and Chile, and were able to build on the native people's fascination with the music of the mass that contrasted greatly with their own lively dances and songs.

The first Spanish music introduced was chiefly vocal in character, but with the later expeditions and particularly the arrival of the Viceroys to administer what had become an empire, there came instrumentalists: trumpeters and drummers, string and wind instrument players. With official encouragement from Spain they helped establish a school of music at Texcoco in 1526 and a dancing school in Mexico City in 1528, where the printing of music was started in the 1530s only forty years after Columbus's first voyage. By 1600 seven books of music had been printed, forty years before the publishing of the New England *Bay Psalm Book*, which contained words only (the music for this was not added until 1698). This tremendous achievement owed much to the influence of the very high musical standards of the mother cathedral in Seville and the work of Spanish composers.

Gradually, Spanish composition was influenced by the American tradition, which came to Spain through her returning seaborne envoys and sailors.

Early French voyages also had a missionary and colonising character. Jean de Béthencourt made voyages to the Canary Islands in 1402 and 1405, and deliberately took professional musicians on the latter voyage with the aim of enhancing the quality of life in the new colony. They also assisted missionary work and the establishment of two parishes. In 1503 Paul de Gonneville led a missionary expedition from Honfleur to Brazil on which drummers and trumpeters were carried. It is recorded that they helped with a big religious ceremony in Brazil at Easter 1504. Natives were brought back to demonstrate their tradition and to learn from exposure to the culture of France.[24]

For a variety of reasons the English did not become seriously involved in the rivalry for empire and dominion of the seas until the second half of the sixteenth century, by which time the art of music in England had been greatly fostered by the examples set by the Tudor courts of Henry VII and his son Henry VIII. At this time music was used chiefly to give emphasis and ornament to ceremonies and special events. Thus when Henry VIII travelled to meet Francis I of France at the Field of the Cloth of Gold in 1520, William Cornyshe, an accomplished musician who was Master of the Children of the Chapel Royal, took ten children to sing in the royal choir and was paid expenses for 'the diette of ten children, every of them at 2d the day for sixty-two dais at the Kings journey to Calais'. At Henry's departure from Dover trumpets and drums were played aboard his fine fleet of warships. During the celebrations in France and at the court in London, music would have been played on the softer toned lutes, harps, recorders and perhaps shawms to accompany the maskings, mummings and disguisings.[25]

There is an interesting sidelight on the initiative and enterprise of English sea-going professional musicians in the career of William Crane, who served afloat as a member of the King's Musick and a favourite of Henry VIII. He attended the Field of the Cloth of Gold and became Master of the Children of the Chapel Royal in about 1525, after William Cornyshe. At the same time he pursued another salty career, for in 1509 he had been appointed water bailiff of the town and port of Dartmouth. He also received money for cables and ship repairs and in an Exchequer account of 1513 is described as 'William Crane, Master of the works of his new ship at Wolwiche'. This was for the repair and rigging of the king's ship the *Carryke* at Woolwich. Similar accounts show him as 'Controller during pleasure, of the tonnage and poundage of the petty custom in the Port of London'' Clearly William Crane had diverse talents and his seaborne music influenced others besides the king.[26]

For his voyage to England to marry Queen Mary Tudor in 1554, Philip II of Spain embarked a group of musicians including trumpeters, drummers, fifers, and other instrumentalists who are unspecified. On the return journey, these amounted to the sixteenth-century equivalent of an orchestra. Travelling in the Marquis de Santa Cruz's galley the King had for his entertainment players of shawms, sackbuts, cornets, dulzians or curtals, recorders, crumhorns, special mountain horns and 'chirimias', who could play a wide range of music from the serious to folk music for dancing. In addition his choir were present to sing whatever might be commanded.[27]

This most cultured monarch was following in the tradition set by earlier European monarchs such as Henry V of England who took a large choir on his travels for his own religious and secular music and to impress others. During the reign of Philip II much encouragement was given to music and it is interesting to note that a mass was composed in 1572 in celebration of the naval victory over the Turks at Lepanto. Also music was often played by large groups on board ship for special occasions. Salutes aboard ship were given by trumpet and drum and by shouts of acclamation.[28]

During Mary's brief reign, English seamen benefited from the links with Spain which had been re-established following her marriage to Philip. Members of officially approved missions visited Seville, and met the persons who controlled the Spanish voyages of exploration and the teaching of navigation. Thus the English built on the knowledge gained earlier in the reign of Edward VI when the Venetian-born Sebastian Cabot[29] came to England to teach the latest methods of navigation. The result was that by the beginning of Elizabeth I's reign in 1558 England was deeply involved in the business of maritime exploration, sending out ships and men in an effort to expand her trading links and her commercial strength. Amongst the many subsequent English voyages, especially those in search of the North-West Passage, are those of Sir Humphrey Gilbert and John Davis.

The loss of Gilbert's largest ship, the *Delight,* in late August of 1583 during his second expedition has a dramatic, almost grand operatic, character about it. Gilbert and the other ships of his flotilla had sailed from Plymouth in June of that year. In the words of Captain Haies of the *Golden Hinde:*

> We were in number in all about 260 men; among whom we had of every faculty good choice, as Shipwrights, Masons, Carpenters, Smiths and such like, requisite to such an action; also mineral men and refiners. Besides for solace of our people and allurment of the savages we were provided of Musike in good variety; not omitting the least toys as Morris dancers, Hobby horses and Maylike concerts to delight the savage people, whom we intended to winne by all faire meanes possible.

On 27 August off Sable Island near Newfoundland, the mood on board the ships changed from alert expectancy to intense, Wagnerian drama and tragedy:

> The evening was fair and pleasant, yet not without token of storm to ensue, and most past of this Wednesday night, like the Swanne that singeth before her death, they in the *Admirall* or *Delight* continued in sounding of trumpets, with Drummes and Fifes; also winding the Cornets, Haughtboyes; and in the end of their jollities left with battell and ringing of doleful knells.

A storm was brewing and they were close to treacherous shoal water and sandbanks. Natural omens such as shoals of porpoises circling round were foreboding. The storm broke on the 29th with a fog over the shallow waters, which hampered vision. The *Delight* struck and all hands were lost. The others who had been able to save themselves kept a vigilant watch and continued to play instruments, but all was in vain. Their companions were gone.

Some two years later, John Davis's expedition left Dartmouth in the *Sunshine* and *Moonshine* with four musicians embarked, who were taken for much the same reasons as those who sailed with Gilbert. They proved a valuable addition for, at Gilbert Sound on 29 July, the natives worried some expedition members who had landed, by making a great clamour that sounded warlike:

> Whereupon Mr Bruton, and the master of his ship, with others
> of their company made great haste towards us, and brought
> our Musicians with them from our shippe, purposing either by
> force to rescue us, if neede should so require, or with curtesie
> to allure the people.[30]

In the end music and courtesy won. The natives left happily and the explorers returned to their ships safely.

The Armada and After

Raids by Sir Francis Drake and others on the sailing ship routes and trading posts established by Spain, plus religious differences, led the two countries into armed conflict and the highly organised but ill-fated Spanish attempt to invade England with the support of the great Armada.

The struggle between England and Spain continued with the English attacking Spanish convoys and ports. In 1589 an expedition to destroy the remaining ships of the Armada sheltering in northern Spain and to take Lisbon was mounted under the leadership of Sir John Norris and Sir Francis Drake. Amongst the latter's outstanding abilities as a fighting seaman was his clear appreciation of the power of music to set men's pulses running and to maintain their morale. He arranged with the Mayor and Council of Norwich to take the City's Waits on the expedition for this purpose. They were given special clothing and new instruments, and their transport by wagon to the port of embarkation was paid for by the City. Regrettably, we have not yet uncovered a detailed account of their part in the expedition, only the knowledge that the expedition was partially successful and that many men died, including three of the five Waits.[31]

In 1591 a professional musician, Thomas Tomkins, the elder of two sons of Thomas Tomkins senior, Precentor of Gloucester Cathedral, sailing in the *Revenge*, took part in an even more celebrated action, when Lord Thomas Howard and the captain of the *Revenge*, Sir Richard Grenville, with other ships attacked a rich Spanish flota off the Azores.[32] The English were beaten but Sir Richard Grenville gained undying-fame by fighting his ship until forced to abandon her as she sank beneath him. Tomkins was amongst those killed on this glorious but tragic occasion.

The Waits were officially paid by the town in one way or another and had various duties as watchmen, sounding the time of night, warnings of approaching danger, the arrival of important people or even of fighting in the town. They also provided officially sponsored entertainment.

The butt of much humour and of strafings by Church authorities for their licentious behaviour, the town musicians nevertheless included some fine players who could achieve very significant results, such as Thomas Farmer and John Ravenscroft in England. The town musicians formed themselves into guilds which gained certain privileges and power and from their records and those of the municipalities, we can gain an insight into their music and instruments, and so of the music played afloat. Stringed instruments were used in Exeter and Chester, but Italian musicians were usually woodwind and brass players. In Germany, town bands included shawms (oboes), cornetts, bassoons, and sackbuts (trombones). In England, Morley's *Consort Lessons*, published in 1599 and the first printed book to mention the London Waits, indicates they played 'A Double Curtall [bassoon], a Lyserden [tenor cornett], a treble oboe, a cornett and a set of records'.

Monarchs and Music at Sea

Another European monarch who had a great interest in music was Christian IV of Denmark, to whom the well-known English musician, John Dowland, was appointed lutenist in 1598 and later sailed with him. Earlier, in 1563 in preparation for the seven years' war against Sweden, the Danish monarch had ordered all towns in Jutland, 'to send a barber with a chest and equipment; and one piper and one drummer to Copenhagen to the Admiral Peter Skram for use in the warships that are being equipped.'[33]

In England the seaman had become a popular figure, especially after the successful repulse of the Spanish Armada. Ordinary folk had had it brought home to them with a jolt that their trade and even national survival depended on ships and seamen, and they began to celebrate their feelings in verse and song. Many ballads commemorating the Armada fight were registered at Stationers' Hall for publication in the second half of 1588, but few have survived. Amongst these is 'A Joyful New Ballad', to the tune of 'Monsieurs Almaigne' by Thomas Deloney of Norwich, and 'Sir Francis Drake; or Eighty Eight', by an unidentified writer. Deloney also wrote, 'The Winning of Cales', in celebration of the taking of Cadiz in 1596. There is another ballad celebrating the exploits of George Clifford, 3rd Earl of Cumberland, who commanded the *Bonaventure* in the English fleet, and which, it was claimed, was still sung in his native Skipton in the 1920s.

The dawn of the new century saw many changes in the course of European maritime history. In England the great queen Elizabeth I died in 1603, but not before granting the East India Company a charter in 1600 and seeing the first of its trading fleets sail direct to India in 1601. Thereby England initiated a profitable trade which was to have as yet unforeseen imperial consequences. At the same time this move stirred a rivalry with the Netherlands, whose merchants were already founding trading 'factories', and with Portugal, whose interests were well established since the voyage of Vasco da Gama in 1497–8.

Elizabeth's successor, James I, made peace with Spain, but reduced his Navy Royal to a reserve fighting force, so exposing English ports and merchant shipping to the attacks of privateers from France and elsewhere. In a move to quench this loss of vital business and esteem, his son, Charles I, introduced a national tax, Ship Money, to pay for a new defensive navy. Amongst other vessels he built the first 100-gun ship, the *Sovereign of the Seas*, the finest fighting ship of her day. However, he lost his throne in his struggle with Parliament for control of the nation and its fighting services.

Charles was a great patron of the arts, including music, and as befitted his royal position, trumpeters attended him during his voyages. We find a bill for attendance in 1628, and in 1631 three farthings was paid *per diem* for Josias Broome, Sergeant Trumpeter and thirteen other trumpeters to attend upon His Majesty at Portsmouth and Rochester when visiting his naval forces. There is also a very interesting entry of a warrant dated 10 May 1632 for 15 shillings *per diem* from 1 April for the 'diet and lodging of Signior Antonio van Dik [van Dyke] and his servants' during their travels. On 7 June 1638 there is a warrant for a 'sea livery' for John Smith, one of His Majesty's trumpeters, and his man, appointed to go to sea 'in his Majesty's great ship called the *Souveraigne*'. This is only one year after the building of the ship.[34]

The need for regulation of this strengthened naval service is reflected in the publication in 1627 of John Smith's *A Sea Grammar*, which includes what may be the earliest regulations in English for musicians afloat:

> The Trumpeter is always to attend the Captain's command and to sound either at his going ashore or comming aboard; at the enter-tainment of strangers; also when you hale a ship, when you charge, boord or enter; and the poope is his place to stand or sit upon.

This summarises the duties which by then had become traditionally those of the trumpeter, and which later were to be taken over by the bosun's call and the bugler.

By comparison, in the fleet of the Danish king Christian IV in 1610, music had reached a higher degree of sophistication:

> On the royal ship there were twelve musicians on board; on a common frigate not less than three. Their instruments were a [? bassoon], trombone, crumborn, shawm, lute and drum played in several tones [in their different parts] in concert. Their most important task was to blow the trumpets in foggy weather. They played hymns, which could show where in the fog the other ships in the convoy were situated. On departing from a foreign harbour the trumpets called the people on board. The Musicians also played at the divine services and when the jour-ney was over and the ships entered the harbour of Copenhagen after the voyage they played a thanksgiving song.[35]

We find some more detail in an account of Christian IV's voyage in his ship *Justinian* to attend an assembly held in Bergen in 1622:

> When eating dinner or supper they sounded kettledrums and blew trumpets by four men ... On our ship were twenty-eight bodyguards and twelve musicians. These two groups had each a big cabin on board.[36]

One notes that two types of ensemble are included, one equipped with trumpets and drums for parade and naval occasions and another with softer toned instruments for leisure entertainment. What could be closer to the duties of Royal Marine musicians in the Royal Navy today, except that they do not have to act as musical foghorns!

In France in the 1600s there was an equivalent interest in dancing and music in the Marine de Guerre:

> Three or four times a week, the ball (the word just signifies dance) takes place amongst seamen and petty officers, and consists of songs, games, combats, climbing competitions to the top of the mast, when bets are laid on the slowest (in principle and without commitment, all betting being forbidden even in the dansette), the speed of which stupefies landsmen.[37]

The king of France also ensured that his ambassador was suitably accompanied when afloat. On his journey to the Bilager wedding in Copenhagen, Charles Ogier embarked in the barge of the commandant of the great castle of Kronborg at Elsinore:

> In the prow stood our superb trumpeter whom the King [of France] had given the ambassador, and he led a French Hymn of Thanksgiving which sounded over the Danish Skanien coasts.[38]

The English Civil War broke out in 1642 and the fleet defected to join the Parliamentary side, because, whilst the king had seen the need to build warships and to make them the finest of their day, he had rather neglected to pay and feed the seamen who manned them. The Parliamentary party and later the Commonwealth and Cromwell saw the absolute requirement for a navy to protect English maritime trade from French and Dutch attack, and built up a new force with a new breed of officers, some taken from the army. The pressing need for this force was soon apparent, because trading rivalry developed into open warfare with the Dutch and to three great naval wars, in which large fleets fought pitched battles.

At the time of the restoration of the monarchy in 1660, Samuel Pepys (1633–1703), the great diarist and naval administrator, was Secretary to Sir Edward Montague, the naval officer who was chiefly responsible for swinging the loyalty of the fleet, of which he was Commander-in-Chief, to the King. Pepys sailed with Sir Edward aboard the *Naseby* with the ships that would bring the King back from the Netherlands to England. He recorded that by way of preparation for the great moment of the King's arrival on board, the Commander-in-Chief inspected his ship and gave orders for musicians.

> My Lord went this morning about the flagship in a boat, to see what alterations there must be, as to the arms and flags. He did give me order also to write for silk flags and scarlett waist cloathes. For a rich barge; for a noise of trumpets, and a set of fidlers.[39]

The position of the trumpeter as the official musician at sea remained unchanged and was enhanced after the Restoration, when there were many more appointments. In 1666 four trumpeters were appointed to attend upon HRH Prince Rupert and the Duke of Albemarle at sea. In the same year a new official sea instrument appeared. On 22 June a warrant was issued, 'to pay Walter Vanbright, his Majesty's Kettledrummer, the sum of £10 for his present supply, he being to attend his Highness Prince Rupert and His Grace the Duke of Albemarle at sea.' There was also a warrant for a sea livery for him.[40]

On 30 January 1672 we find a bill for seven swords, with near silver gilt handles, for six trumpeters and a kettledrummer to attend Lord Duras into France. The welfare of the trumpeters' families was also carefully attended to, as we see from a Letter of Assignment from William Porter dated 7 December 1675: 'one of the pentioner trumpeters of His Majesty, now bound out to sea in the East Indies in the good ship called *Loyall Eagle*, appointing his daughter, Prudence Porter, his true and lawful attorney'. The same William Porter was left at St Helena on the way home in 1677 to recover his health.[41]

In 1682 Gervaise Price, 'His Majesty's Sergeant Trumpeter', received an authority to obtain four silver trumpets to replace those lost at sea. Perhaps the most distinguished trumpeter was William Shore, appointed to Charles II's service in 1679. He became Sergeant Trumpeter in 1683: 'Sergeant of the trumpeters drummers and fifes in ordinary to His Majesty with the right to collect a fee of $1/2$d per day from every player of the trumpet, drum or fife at public performances or an annual licence of 20/−'. In 1684 he became the first to occupy the Public Professorship of Music at Cambridge University and in 1691 he went to sea to accompany William III on his voyage to the Netherlands and back; in 1697 he made a similar voyage to accompany ambassadors to the Treaty of Ryswick.[42]

Enter the Royal Marines

In Britain, 1664 is an important year in the annals of official naval music, for it marks the establishment of a new regiment of sea soldiers or marines, the Royal Marines as we now call them. First established by James, Duke of York (later James II), who was Lord High Admiral to his brother Charles II and who fought at sea in a number of actions, the regiment was then called the Duke of York and Albany's or Lord High Admiral's Regiment. They were disbanded and reformed in 1703, since when they have played an outstandingly valorous and important part in our British naval history, not least because of the very high standard of their music which was a feature from their earliest days.

William III who, with his wife Mary II, came to the throne after the flight of the unfortunate and politically inept James II, united and reinvigorated the navies of England and the Netherlands, to fight the menacing fleet of France. In 1691 he had already appointed trumpeters, oboists and drummers to his Guards, Grenadiers and Horse Guards. It followed naturally that the re-established marine regiment should have fifes and drums too. In William's fleet the importance of music was recognised, as is reflected in the private publication of a series of *Dialogues* about the management of warships and naval life, written by N Boteler (1577–c. 1640) and published posthumously in 1685 and 1688. The *Dialogues* are between an admiral and a captain and it is worth quoting certain passages about the use of trumpets and whistles in full:

> CAPTAIN. After the Cook comes the Coxswain, and he is to have the peculiar charge of the barge or shallop belonging to the ship, and of all the implements; and so be ready with his boat and boat's company or gang of men, either to wait upon the Captain, or any person of fashion that the Captain shall appoint to be fetched from the shore, or carried thither or anywhere else; and he is to see her trimmed with her carpet and cushions, and to be in person himself in the stern, with his silver whistle to cheer up his gang; and with his hand to steer the boat; and to keep his men together when he goeth to the shore. And this is the lowest officer in a ship that wears a whistle.

> ADMIRAL. How many be the officers that carry whistles in a ship of war?

> CAPTAIN. They are three: The Master, the Boatswain, and the Coxswain, for though the Captain may do the same at his pleasure, yet it is neither usual, nor necessary.

> Notice therefore being given that upon such a day, the Prince himself, or his High Admiral of the Kingdoms, or some General of a present fleet, intendeth to visit any of his chief ships before they go out to sea; and that his pleasure is to be publicly, and with ceremony, received aboard. By the break of that day, the ship is in every part to be made neat and clean, and to be trimmed with all her ensigns and pendants; the ship's barge is early in the morning to be sent from the ship to the shore, perfectly furnished with carpets, cushions, tilt, and the like; the Coxswain with his whistle and best clothes being to attend in the stern, and the barge's gang in their liveries to row. Upon the more near approach of the barge, the ship's noise of trumpets are to sound; and so to hold on until the barge come within less than musket shot of the ship. And then the trumpets are to cease; and all such as carry whistles are to whistle a welcome three several times; and in every interim the ship's whole company are to hail the barge with a joint shout, after the custom of the sea.

> As soon as the whistles and shouts of salute and welcome are stilled, the trumpets are again to sound a welcome to the ship's side.[43]

In the rival Marine de Guerre of Louis XIV of France, we find in the *Ordonnances du Roi Concernant les Gardes du Pavillon et de la Marine et des Volontaires* of 1689, provision for musical instruments for the Gardes, the equivalent of the Royal Marines. It is interesting to note also a special development in the French Marine:

> Article 61. There will be maintained in the ports of Brest, Toulon and Rochefort for the instruction of the Gardes … Masters of Mathematics, Hydrography, Drawing, Ship Construction, Fencing and Dancing …

This must be the first mention of the official recognition of the importance of dancing at sea in a navy. It is typical of the French love of culture and education, and their wish to see their people and seamen well educated, that full training in many branches of seamanship and associated skills was provided in this way. This provision was confirmed in the *Ordonnances* of 1764 and 1765.

Special provision is made for trumpeters for admirals and captains when aboard their ships. Some senior officers had had such musicians as early as 1671, but these were less formal appointments, although retention of the services of a good trumpeter was seen as very important for prestige and French admirals got into bitter quarrels about such matters.

One way of resolving such time-wasting rivalries was for the state to fund the provision of an adequate number of trained musicians. In this way groups of musicians could be recruited to play on board naval ships to meet the increasing demand for music on ceremonial and other occasions, thus replacing the small number of trumpeters and drummers usually appointed from naval sources or from among royal musicians. Gradually this happened, as will be seen in the next chapter, but the process was slow moving and required the pressure of international warfare on a grand scale and the build-up of nationalist sentiments to give it a real impetus. Meanwhile, many battles were to be fought with or without musicians.

Trumpeters play aboard a French warship of c.1680. Drawing attributed to Puget.

3 Strike up the Band

Sound, sound the clarion, fill the fife,
Throughout the sensual world proclaim,
One crowded hour of glorious life
Is worth an age without a name.

Thomas Osbert Mordaunt, The Bee

While music was perhaps not the deciding factor in battles at sea, an action was sometimes heralded by aggressive competitive fanfares, as in a certain incident in the Far East. The forces of two old trading rivals, the Netherlands and Portugal, were fighting each other at Macao, the European trading post permitted by the Chinese. The Dutch were trying to capture the Portuguese fort by a seaborne landing and reckoned they had the upper hand after distracting the defenders' attention with a fierce daytime bombardment from three ships:

> The ships drew off at sunset, but celebrated the expected victory by blowing trumpets and beating drums all night. Not to be outdone by this bravado, Lopo Sarmento de Carvalho ordered similar martial rejoicings to be made on the city's bulwarks 'so that the enemy should understand that we had greater reason to rejoice, by the manifold mercies which our Lord God had shown us.' Since it was obvious that the enemy would land next day, Lopo Sarmento spent the night in visiting all the fortified posts and exhorting the soldiers and citizens to fight to the last. He pointed out that they could expect no mercy from their heretic foes, nor seek refuge with the Chinese, the majority of whom had abandoned the town.[44]

Lopo Sarmento's response to the musical challenge of the would-be invaders resulted in the defeat of the Dutch and the Portuguese were left to increase their trade and influence.

Meanwhile from another European country, Sweden, we have evidence of the instruments played in warships, discovered by marine archaeologists. This evidence from a flagship, complements the naval musical establishment of Sweden's rivals, the Danes and of their King, Christian IV. I refer to the excavation in 1980–81 of the Royal Swedish flagship *Kronan*, which sank on 1 June 1676 off the east coast island of Öland in a sea battle with the Danes. Amongst the many thousands of finds are several musical instruments. These are violins, drums, trumpets, bass viola da gamba, a whistle and parts of home-made seamen's fiddles. One of the trumpets comes from Nuremberg, a city famous for such instruments and is signed and dated Michael Nagel, 1654. It is known that kettledrums were also carried and it is quite likely that other instruments such as transverse flute, trombone, theorbo, recorder, and double bass, even perhaps a harpsichord, were on board in port.[45]

Of course the *Kronan* was a particularly important ship and, as such, had a special complement of musicians, but one notes the same combination of instruments as found in the Danish flagship. Some, like the drums and trumpets would have been used principally for naval ceremonial and warlike purposes, the others for entertainment, probably in the company of guests.

Careful research has been done in southern Sweden on the kinds of music that were almost certainly played on board. These were fairly wide ranging and consisted of lieder, dance music such as gavottes and allemandes, sonatas and chaconnes.

British Naval Bands are Born

In many European countries, wars, revolutions and, in the case of Germany, the nineteenth-century campaign of unification, interrupted the history of naval bands drastically, but it can be clearly traced in the story of Britain's Royal Marines, which have a continuous history of more than 300 years. A close rival is the United States Marine Band, which can trace its history back to a small fife and drum band that marched on the streets of Philadelphia in November 1775. In Britain, two main threads are interwoven. Firstly, the provision of music on board seagoing ships, which at first was shared between the Royal Navy and the Royal Marines. Secondly, the need for music in land bases, which was met by the Royal Marines.

When the Corps of Marines was eventually established on a permanent basis in 1775, it was formed into three Grand Divisions, which were housed at barracks in Chatham, Portsmouth and Plymouth. The barracks provided quarters suited to the establishment of bands, which would include an ensemble of instruments related to that provided for a German military band, known as a Harmonie Musick. These included oboes, clarinets, horns and bassoons, a much wider range than before. The exact date of the establishment of bands is uncertain, but Portsmouth had one by 1763, Plymouth by 1767 and Chatham by 1772. The title 'Royal' was granted in 1802.[46] After 1805 a fourth division of the Royal Marines was formed at Woolwich, to which Deal was added in 1861, whence musicians were appointed to serve at sea. In 1862 the Marines were formed into two branches, the Royal Marines Light Infantry and the Royal Marines Artillery. The latter had its own band service and provided bands for the Royal Yachts, after a decision made by King Edward VII in 1903. The two branches were amalgamated into the single Corps of Royal Marines in 1923.

At sea in the late eighteenth century the Marines would normally provide the official drummer on board and, depending on the size of the unit, would have had a fife and drum band with youngsters as instrumentalists, who in battle had other duties such as supplying marksmen with ammunition. When the ship to which they were appointed was put out of commission, musicians would return to their barracks on land for further training.

Ashore, each division had its own band and the competition between them was intense. The circumstances leading to the creation of each band were different, but a common feature seems to have been the officers' need

Royal Marines with their boy drummer stand guard (far left) as a seaman is about to be punished with a flogging, 1825. Engraving by J Robins, after G Cruikshank's 'The Point of Honor'.

for entertainment in their Mess, where the members would subscribe towards the cost of instruments, music and pay. Early examples of the duties of Royal Marines bands are the order for the Chatham band to attend George III's review of the Fleet at Spithead in 1773, and the Portsmouth band playing at Lord Howe's return to Portsmouth in 1794, after the Battle of the 'Glorious First of June'.

Playing at important national events such as coronations and royal funerals, attending the sovereign or the Prince of Wales on a royal tour or, in the case of Queen Victoria, playing at her home, Osborne House in the Isle of Wight, were amongst the many duties performed by the bands. In 1826 the Chatham band attended the coronation of Tsar Nicholas I of Russia in the suite of the British ambassador, and was the first British band ever to perform at a foreign ceremony in this way. These important occasions gave opportunities for the musicians to show their prowess and for both the bands and bandmasters to be rewarded by promotion and the award of special badges or medals for excellence. In addition to these events, the bands would play regularly and often daily at parades, church services, and in the evenings at the officers' Mess. The life was demanding, but it bred bandsmen and bandmasters of exceptionally good quality, who fully deserved the royal patronage bestowed on them. Examples are Captain Charles Hoby, who became Professor of Military Music at the Royal College of Music in 1920; Major Frederick J Ricketts, who, under his *nom de plume* of Kenneth Alford, became a famous composer of march tunes; Captain R P O'Donnell, who served as a Director of Music or Bandmaster in all three services; and Lieutenant V Dunn, later Lieutenant-Colonel Sir Vivian Dunn.

From their beginning, Royal Marines bands were trained to perform both military marching music with wind and percussion instruments, and music for entertainment, with stringed instruments, at service dinners or public concerts for example. Their special position as sea-going musicians, away from home contacts, meant that they had to play both kinds of music, often in difficult, crowded circumstances or on important occasions of state.

The development of instrumentation for Royal Marines bands follows the general history of instruments, but particular mention must be made of certain points. Firstly, there was the ghastly shambles at Scutari in 1854 during the Crimean War, when the massed bands of the British Army played the National Anthem, but with each regiment having a different score and playing at a different pitch. The consequence of this ear shattering event was the foundation of the Royal Military School of Music at Kneller Hall and the standardisation of the pitch of British military music. In 1929 this was fixed at the low or universal concert pitch of A = 439 cycles per second.

Another important point was the invention of keys and then valves for brass instruments. Without these, brass instruments were limited to the primitive harmonies of their fixed tubing; crudely speaking the sort of notes that can be obtained from blowing down a length of brass tube, which are limited in range and quality. The invention in 1810 of the kent-bugle with five keys and then the ophicleide a few years later extended the range of brass instruments so that they could play melodic line instead of providing a background accompaniment only. This situation was improved enormously with the invention of the valve for brass instruments. Much is owed to the inventive mind of Adolphe Sax, who in the 1840s developed the saxhorn and saxophone families of instruments. By the 1860s bands were, in general, equipped with the cornet and euphonium, although it was not until thirty years later that saxophones were accepted in naval bands. Meanwhile clarinets, oboes and bassoons remained favourite and permanent members of the band family. The size of bands evolved from the usual ten or twelve at the end of the eighteenth century, to an official twenty-two for Royal Marines divisional bands in 1815. Nowadays twenty-five is considered appropriate, but bands can be much larger for special concerts or parades and can play a very wide range of music.

Adolphe Sax (1814–94), Belgian inventor of the saxophone and the saxhorn family of instruments.

In days gone by, bands were specifically recruited to play on board ship at sea and were originally manned by naval, not marine personnel. They were the direct descendants of the trumpeters who enjoyed such an honourable role in the story of maritime music. Trumpeters had become part of the officially 'rated', graded if you like, members of a ship's company, but by 1731 were beginning to lose their status and by 1816 were phased out of naval rankings and rates of pay. They were reinstated in 1839 and from 1842 were rated as Musicians.[47]

Early ships' bands were made up of musicians with or without sea-going experience, recruited directly for service in a ship on the initiative of individual captains or admirals. Their pay as ordinary seamen was enchanced by money from the private pockets of senior officers. Consequently, they were only paid during the commission of a ship. When the ship went out of

Amongst the ship's company of HMS Coquette of 1855 are seamen with their fiddle, fife and drum, as well as their pet monkeys.

commission, the musicians, like the vast majority of the seamen, were out of work until they could find another ship. This system was altered when in 1847 the Admiralty introduced the rate of continuous service Bandsman with proper pay and pension, and determined the size of band each type of ship should carry, but continuous service was not compulsory and some musicians remained on non-continuous service, which was a cause of trouble.

Training for boy musicians was introduced in 1860–62, and for the first time funds for purchasing instruments were provided by the Admiralty, but only for training purposes. In 1863 the senior ratings of Bandmaster and Chief Bandmaster were introduced, giving a proper career structure for the long service man. This was the first official use of the rank of Bandmaster. In 1874 it was suddenly realised that naval bandsmen had no official uniform, so one was devised forthwith, which had white trimmings on a dark blue cloth and an unseamanlike pill box cap. This rig led to the wearers being called the 'Hamoaze Hussars', after the Plymouth anchorage where training ships were moored.

In 1883 the average ship's band consisted of eleven men who could double as a wind or string band, and in 1890 their uniform was altered to a more suitable pattern. The first shore establishment to have a band was HMS *Excellent* in 1895, the training ship for gunners at Portsmouth.

Purchase of instruments and music, plus general maintenance expenses of ships' bands still depended largely on the private pockets of senior officers

Aboard HMS Lion *of 1896 a Royal Marines band with Royal Navy buglers, stands ready to accompany a landing party on exercise.*

and this could be a considerable burden, which gradually became unacceptable. In addition, the non-continuous service musicians proved a thorn in the side of naval discipline, because they were often foreign-born men who did not show the same respect for order as the British seamen. This unsatisfactory situation led to an official memorandum being presented to Parliament in 1902 and the formation of a whole new service in 1903.[48]

In Tune with the Twentieth Century

Under the 1903 scheme the Royal Marines became responsible for providing all naval music for the Royal Navy, with the title of Royal Marines

Seamen dancing to a makeshift band aboard HMS Edinburgh, *c.1885.*

Band Service. Further, a Royal Navy School of Music (RNSM) was created: it remained in being until 1950. By 1912 the School had more than 400 students and at the outbreak of the First World War there were some fifty-three bands serving in different parts of the world. Following war service, the fortunes of the Band Service and of the RNSM followed patterns not dissimilar to those experienced throughout all the services. Stringent cuts forced reductions in pay and restrictions on equipment. More seriously, trained musicians began to leave because of domestic problems that arose from long periods of service at sea. Whilst the strength of the service in 1939 was put at 1,400 men, some 370 of these were boys in training. Out of the 1,000 remaining, bands were being provided for ships in about twenty-four different parts of the world as well as for shore establishments. At the outbreak of the Second World War, all available retired musicians were recalled to the colours and extras were recruited from civilian sources to cover the wide-spread demands of a rapidly increasing service.

Meanwhile, in 1930, the RNSM had moved from its original home at Eastney to better accommodation at Deal, where it remained until 1996. It was in the 1930s also that the custom of Beating Retreat, a military ceremony some 400 years old, was introduced on special occasions by the Commander-in-Chief of the Mediterranean Fleet. As a culminating and moving feature, a special setting of the Sunset Call, arranged by Fleet Bandmaster A C Green, was played as the White Ensign was lowered. This was first performed at Gibraltar in 1934 and has since become a favourite piece of naval music, recognised as a special hallmark of the RM Band Service.

After the Second World War the Service had to adjust to the large scale reductions in the Armed Services, as they were gradually put on a peacetime footing. The Service also had to face a problem that was peculiarly its own. This was the rival existence of the old divisional bands, who now chiefly provided ceremonial music on a grand scale ashore, and the ships' bands trained by the RNSM, whose musicians served much of their time afloat. Conditions were much more favourable for the divisional bands than for the ships' bands and there was a certain professional antagonism between the two. As part of the overall manpower cuts for the Royal Marines, a unified Band Service based on the renamed Royal Marines School of Music at Deal was created on 1 September 1950. The divisional bands were maintained for a while, but with further reductions in the Service generally, and the closure of Chatham Royal Marines barracks in 1950, they became staff bands attached to the various flag officers' commands, the Commando Training Centre, the RN College at Dartmouth and so forth. The continuing appointment of ships' bands was directed from Deal. Today a reduced Band Service still maintains the highest standards of naval music, to the great benefit of the Royal Navy and of the civilian population in general.

The high musical standard of the RM Bands in peace and war has always been matched by their gallant and distinguished service in action. One of their traditional, often dangerous, tasks in battle is to act as stretcher bearers. They have also had duties at communication points aboard ships, where they have stood watch for long hours in very uncomfortable conditions. With the development of sophisticated gunnery control systems, it became the task of bandsmen to operate the delicate controls of the transmitting station in the heart of the ship, where observations were received and orders passed on by instruments to fire the guns. The task required absolute fingertip control and firm discipline, for the effectiveness of the ship's guns and hence her fighting efficiency depended on this. It was a task for which Royal Marines bandsmen were admirably suited and which they carried out in the Second World War with the greatest success, as described by C S Forester in his book, *The Ship*.[49] At the same time bands were still required to play at ceremonials and at concerts, both planned and impromptu, in order to boost morale and maintain effort even under the worst conditions. There are many stories illustrating this. One relates how the Commander-in-Chief Mediterranean, Admiral A B Cunningham, later Lord Cunningham of Hyndhope, insisted on holding a full morning colours ceremony at 6.00 a.m. aboard his flagship HMS *Queen Elizabeth*, despite the fact that she had been damaged by Italian midget submarine attack, was in danger of sinking and that the deck was heeling with a 15° list. Another tells of the band from HMS *Penelope* at Malta playing on board a lighter moored alongside a merchant ship whose precious cargo of oil and fuel was being unloaded in the midst of an enemy air raid. Despite continuous bombing the band played from 9.00 a.m. to 4.00 p.m. for two days to encourage the successful unloading of the ship. On another occasion five musicians aboard HMS *Cleopatra* played on deck as she limped into harbour while eleven colleagues lay wounded below. In the Falklands campaign of 1982 the Royal Marines bandsmen only managed to ship their instruments at the very last moment, but their playing proved invaluable for the morale of the British forces and especially for the wounded during painful evacuation periods. This maintained a tradition set many years before, instilling an impression in the minds of those present that would last a lifetime, like the memory that Vice-Admiral W S Lovell retained of the early stages of the Battle of Tragalgar. He was sixteen at the time, having joined the Royal Navy and had gone to sea in his first ship at the age of ten. He wrote in his memoirs:

> Lord Nelson's van was strong – three 3-deckers, viz. *Victory*, *Temeraire* and *Neptune*, and four 74s, their jib-booms nearly over the others' tafrails, the bands playing 'God Save the King', 'Rule Britannia', and 'Britons Strike Home'; the crews stationed on the forecastle of the different ships cheering the ship ahead of them when the enemy began to fire, sent those feelings to our hearts that ensured us victory.[50]

Today there is a greatly reduced call for RM musicians to serve at sea, because compared with the fleet in the 1930s, the Royal Navy, like many other navies, has far fewer large ships with suitable accommodation for a band. The ultimate deterrent is now provided by nuclear submarines.

Where possible and convenient, tape recordings and discs can be played over a ship's internal broadcasting system, providing canned musical entertainment, which can be made into programmes by volunteer disc jockeys. To

The ship's orchestra of HMS Queen Elizabeth, *1916.*

some extent this replaces the band playing for entertainment, but will never achieve the thrilling stimulation given by a live band. The morale boosting effect of hearing and seeing a real band in action remains remarkable. It has to do with one or more musicians communicating with their fellows by playing for and to them, by expressing mutual feelings through the interpretation of inspiring melodies. The mental and emotional processes involved are hard to explain, but they are very strong and can be generated in no other way. There will always be a need and a place for naval musicians even though the location for playing is not so easily found. The Royal Marines Band Service will always meet this need and meet it to the very highest standards.

Lt B S Green and the band of the Royal Yacht Victoria & Albert, *1913.*

Their colleagues in the French Marine de Guerre have had something of a similar history, but this was interrupted by the Revolution of 1789. Although their service received attention and encouragement under Napoleon I, he was

more interested in his army and it was not until later in the nineteenth century that French naval music truly developed. Their story is not dissimilar from
the British, but it is characteristic of French culture, with its great respect for
the Arts, that their music was carefully nurtured and standards were strictly
monitored in collaboration with the Conservatoire in Paris. A particular and,
I believe, unique group is their pipe band, which is still in vigorous existence,
reflecting the strong Breton element in the Marine.

On board the SS
Gothic during the
royal tour of 1953–4
the Royal Marines
band was under the
direction of Lt-Col.
Vivian Dunn.

In Portugal the navy is a favourite service as one might imagine from that
country's long seafaring tradition. The large main band belongs to the
Armada, or navy, the Marine infantry regiments having smaller units. Early
examples of their uniform and drums can be seen in the Museu de Marinha,
Lisbon, dated 1783. Their neighbours, the Spanish, have an important band,
too, but the full history of this remains to be researched.

Getting the Message Across

A vital need, common to all fighting navies is for the captain of a warship to
be able to communicate with his ship's company in even the most difficult
moments of storm and battle. From the 1930s onward, this has been possible
by microphone and loudspeaker, but even in the Second World War, voice
communication by tube was still a common means of giving orders from the
bridge in battle; loudspeakers were a supplementary for general announce-
ments and communications during ordinary cruising. Speaking tubes could
be linked directly to the main controlling parts of the ship, particularly the
engine room, which also had bell telegraphs. Tubes survived damage better
than electrical systems. However, electrical communication was vital for dis-
tant parts of the ship, gun turrets and the like. None of this precluded the
continued use of the boatswain's (bosun's) call and the bugle.

The most characteristic communication instrument and the one that
has lasted longest is the bosun's call. This is a form of whistle made of

metal and specially adapted for seamen's use, being short and worn on a lanyard or special chain slung round the neck, so that it was kept safely but did not encumber men who had to move quickly round the limited spaces of a ship. By stopping or half-stopping the open hole at the end of the call, it is possible to vary the note played, though the range is limited. Trills can be made by using the tongue to control the breath. The bosun's call seems to have come into use in the fourteenth century both as an instrument of command and as a mark of honour. The oldest one at the National Maritime Museum, Greenwich, dates from the early sixteenth century.[51] Special calls with silver chains were given as rewards for meritorious service and in the sixteenth century the Lord High Admiral, Lord Howard of Effingham, was presented with a gold call as a special mark of his rank. The penetrating though not harsh sound of the bosun's call was admirably suited to broadcast wordless instructions on board sailing ships and various 'pipes' were devised to transmit these. The bosun's call was used in English warships and in East India Company ships, but was not used in ordinary merchant ships. As its name implies it was used principally by the boatswain and his mates, but other senior rates might use it when circumstances dictated. The bosun's call is still in use in the Royal Navy, particularly for ceremonies such as that of welcoming a captain or important visitor aboard ship, but much of the communication role of the call in a large ship was taken over in about 1859 by the bugle played by a RM bugler. For this purpose the Royal Marines have a Bugler Branch, which is now an integral part of the RM Band Service, based since 1996 at HMS *Nelson* at Portsmouth. The Branch, which is also responsible for the training of drummers, claims origins back to the seventeenth century fife and drum bands, but use of the drum for shipboard communications was largely dropped in the nineteenth century. The French, however, continued to use the trumpet.

OPPOSITE Hoisting the colours ceremony aboard HMS Tiger, c. 1925.

Late eighteenth-century silver presentation bosun's call, used to call three cheers after the Battle of Camperdown, 1797.

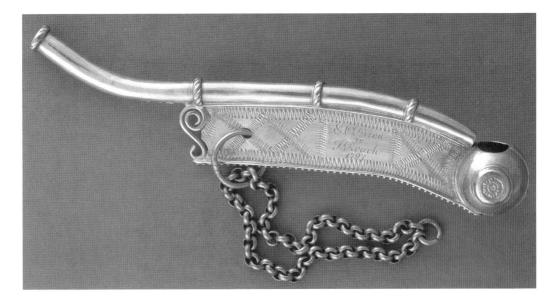

The music played by the earliest marine regiment would have consisted chiefly of marching tunes, but from the late seventeenth century onwards, when in Britain the population at large had more fully realised its dependence on sea trade and on the fighting navy as a defender both of the trade and of the island home, the seaman became a popular folk hero and many ballads were written about him. These and other folk tunes would have been played at sea for leisure and particularly for dancing. The large scale wars of the eighteenth century nurtured feelings of nationalism: patriotic songs and other such pieces were composed, which would also have featured. With the nineteenth-century development of light opera and an abundance of attractive concert music such as a overtures, the repertoire of the marine bands, which now had the appropriate instruments, was extended further.

The twentieth century saw a number of rapid and deeply influencing developments in the business of bringing music to the public at large; the advent of wireless telegraphy and radio broadcasts; the arrival of the gramophone and records; the advent of films with accompanying music; two world wars and the organisation of concerts for the entertainment of Service people and of workers in factories and at home.

The Royal Marines Band Service has kept in step with all these developments and maintained a full programme for the public at large as well as the Royal Navy by playing in concert halls, on bandstands, by recording and broadcasting and appearing on television. The Service

extended its repertoire to include music derived from films, musical theatre and other popular sources.

Sir Malcolm Sargent, who was appointed Honorary Adviser in Music
to the Royal Marines in 1949, gave encouragement to the further development of the repertoire and, in collaboration with Sir Vivian Dunn,
conducted several prestigious concerts, notably in the coronation year.
In 1973, on the intiative of the then Principal Director of Music,
Lieutenant-Colonel Paul Neville, a large-scale concert was given at the
Royal Albert Hall in support of the Royal Academy of Music. This was
so successful that it became an annual event in aid of various charities,
among them the Malcolm Sargent Cancer Fund for Children. The
demand for tickets became so great that the concert had to be repeated
on two, and eventually on three consecutive nights. Following the assas-
sination of Earl Mountbatten of Burma, in 1981 the event was renamed
The Mountbatten Festival of Music.

Although not strictly connected with RM bands, Sir Henry Wood's
Fantasia on British Sea Songs, designed to celebrate the centenary in 1905
of the Battle of Trafalgar, and a long standing feature of the Last Night
of the Proms, is a vivid expression of the enduring popularity of sea
music. Royal Marines bands today can perform music of many kinds at
the highest standard, but perhaps what matters most to many people is
their ability to stir hearts and minds with nautical favourites such as
'Heart of Oak' or the regimental march 'A Life on The Ocean Wave'.

The band plays a concert for the men aboard HMS Rodney *at Scapa Flow in the Second World War.*

4 The Fiddler on the Maindeck

There's many a good tune played on an old fiddle.

Samuel Butler, The Way of All Flesh

The plight of the seasick landlubber has always inspired both amusement and pity in the professional seaman and such was the case in the fifteenth century, as we see from some verses of the time of Henry VI (1421–71). Written by an unidentified seaman, they express the attitude of the captain to the pilgrims to St James of Compostela in northern Spain, who have taken passage in his ship:

> Bestowe the boote, bote-swayne, anon,
> That our pylgryms may pley thereon;
> For som ar lyke to cowgh and grone,
> Or hit be full mydnyght.
> Hale the bowelyne. Now, vere the shete.–
> Cooke, make redy anoone our mete,
> Our pylgryms have no lust to ete, I pray God yeve him rest.

(Tidy up the ship directly bosun so that our pilgrims may relax, for some will probably be sick and groaning before midnight.

Haul on the bowline, slacken the sheet. Cook prepare our meal shortly. Our pilgrims have no wish to eat poor things; I pray God will give them a good night's rest.)[52]

The author's failure to tell us how the pilgrims amused themselves when well enough and whether they had any musical instruments is made good in the beautiful carvings over the portico of St James, the Portico de la Gloria, installed in 1188, which show in great detail the instruments brought by pilgrims. Though the carvings show twelfth- and thirteenth-century instruments, these were still used in the fifteenth century. They include fiddles or vielles of the waisted and pear-shaped type, like a cittern, which were plucked or played with a bow; harps including the Celtic harp; the psaltery, which was like a horizontal harp with a sounding box; lutes and an organistrum, a form of hurdy-gurdy. Fortunately also one of the oldest German songs to have survived with its music is one sung by pilgrims making their way to St James of Compostela. It is entitled 'Wer hie das Elend bauen well' and dates from the same period.[53] Hence, we have a fair idea of what pilgrims played and sang. In his wonderful description of fourteenth-century pilgrims in *The Canterbury Tales*, Geoffrey Chaucer (c. 1340–1400) mentions the same instruments, plus the recorder and bagpipes, both of them popular instruments all over Europe. In 1361 we find that the Hansa towns were equipping a fleet against Valdemaar, King of Denmark and that 'Besides the sailors and soldiers every ship took a doctor, three cooks and three flautists'. Flautist usually means recorder player.

On a more glorious occasion the King of Denmark visited Venice in 1424, where he was received in state. 'A great deputation of noblemen was sent out to welcome the guest and the Doge fetched him in his own state galley, *Il Bucentaure*, whilst an orchestra played on the deck'.[54]

Travelling by sea was a dangerous business. In addition to the natural hazards of storm and seas and the limited knowledge of navigators, there was always the fear of attack by pirates and other enemies. The relief that pilgrims and others must have felt on their safe arrival in port, and the way they expressed this in song is well described in the following note of the Lotheringian wine fleet arriving in London in 1100: 'As soon as they reached the limits of the harbour of London after New Wear [close to Yantlett Creek] the people on board start to tap one of the wine barrels, the so-called tap wine, hoist their flag and sing after the old pious custom, their Kyrie Eleison, until they reach London Bridge'.

Singing was very popular with travellers by sea and land, who picked up a repertoire from the professional minstrels and troubadours, also from the music they heard in church, which developed from the early plainsong chant codified under Pope Gregory during the years 540–604. An example of the kind of song heard by thirteenth and fourteenth-century travellers is the oldest known English round, 'Sumer is icumen in', which has been dated around 1240 and which was probably composed by someone with a religious background, who may have been Walter Odington of Evesham. Although a secular work, it has duplicate words in Latin which indicate that the tune could have been used for religious purposes. There is a similar example in the fifteenth-century German song, 'Eskommt ein Schiff geladen' (a loaded ship is arriving), which uses the metaphor of a heavily laden ship returning home to express a Christian message.[55]

We have already noted the kind of romantic song that the jongleurs probably sang to entertain important passengers aboard a ship of the thirteenth or fourteenth century. An indication of how ladies were entertained at sea is given in a fifteenth-century miniature of the story of Tristan and Iseult. Iseult is being served food and wine, whilst trumpeters play, but she is not singing herself.[56]

The Portuguese seamen who sailed with Vasco da Gama and others on the fifteenth-century pioneering voyages of discovery had amongst them companions who could play their folk instruments for singing and dancing, including the bagpipes from the mountainous regions of northern Portugal. Luis de Cadamosto gives a fascinating and amusing account of how this instrument was received among the natives they encountered:

> They marvelled at the sound of our bagpipes, which had been played by one of my seamen and which were dressed with colours and ribbons; they thought it was a live animal that sang with different voices and they liked it very much and marvelled at the same time; to show them that it was a simple instrument

> I put it into his hands without inflating it; following which they saw it was artificial, but that the playing was divine and that God made the instrument with his own hands, because it played so sweetly and with such a variety of voices, and protested they had never heard anything so charming.[57]
>
> [Author's translation]

The seamen who served in Columbus's ship on his third voyage to the Caribbean in 1498 took tabors, pipes and tambourines to amuse themselves. Columbus ordered them to play and the ship's boys to dance when he was trying to entice the natives of the island of Trinidad, off Venezuela, to communicate with him. Unfortunately, this move had the reverse effect, for the natives decided this gesture of peace was actually the prelude to a fight and fired arrows at the ship in a very hostile manner![58]

Musical Diversions in Tudor Times

Although there is evidence to indicate that as a result of royal interest and the influence of the Reformation and the Renaissance, the playing of music became more of a common pastime amongst the English gentry of the sixteenth century, there is tantalisingly little evidence of the playing of music for leisure aboard ships of the period. One important item, however, is the discovery of the remains of a shawm, (ancestor of the oboe,) two stringed instruments, a tabor (form of drum) and three tabor pipes in the wreck of the English warship, *Mary Rose*, which was swamped and sank on her way to an engagement with the French off Spithead in 1545, and was salvaged in 1982. That the shawm was found in the surgeon's cabin has a particular significance, which will be discussed later in Chapter 6. All the instruments were those normally played for genteel entertainment. The conclusion that such instruments were taken on board important ships carrying senior officers and the gentry is supported by the well-known fact that Sir Francis Drake took viols and players in the *Golden Hind* during his circumnavigation of the globe, 1577–80.[59] He produced them to good effect when he was entertaining an important Spanish prisoner, Francisco de Zarate, who subsequently reported favourably to the Viceroy of Spain in South America: 'His dining and supping is to the music of Vigolones'. Drake was attended by nine or ten gentlemen who, together with the Portuguese pilot, sat with him at table. Thus the gentleman seaman adventurer had his entourage and listened to music even when at sea on a dangerous mission. On arrival in the East Indies, Drake entertained the King of Molucca who, in the words of Hakluyt, 'seemed to be much delighted with the sound of our music'.

Given the number of ships and men involved, and despite the need to concentrate on the fighting, there must have been moments when some music was needed for entertainment during the 1588 great Armada campaign, but on the English side there is no known mention of this. However, in the Spanish fleet musical instruments were carried in addition to the official trumpets, drums and pipes, as has been shown from the excavation of artefacts from the wreck of the *Trinidad Valencera* in Kinagoe Bay, County Donegal, Ireland. She was a Venetian merchant ship converted for war and store-carrying. Amongst the artefacts part of a stringed instrument like a guitar, a tambourine frame and the hexagonal wooden end-pieces of a concertina ornamented in silver were found. On their tense voyage from Spain, and perhaps during their subsequent flight from the English around the north of Scotland and down to the west coast of Ireland, the ship's company must have been glad of some musical light relief.[60]

Rivalry and struggles for superiority in maritime trade have continued into our own time, but these are not altogether negative influences and the many consequent seaborne exchanges of different cultures, including music, have been beneficial. Acceleration of these rivalries occurred in the seventeenth century between three principal European powers, England,

Pipes recovered from the wreck of the Mary Rose, *which sank in 1545.*

France and the Netherlands. Simultaneously and naturally the increase in the volume of trading and in naval activities generated a rise in the fortunes of the so called middle classes, merchants, shipbuilders, shipowners, financiers, insurance brokers and naval administrators. As their social status and power improved, so they took more interest in the arts, including music. They were also more literate than their predecessors and some had the inclination to keep records and diaries of their daily life.

For seventeenth-century maritime England we are fortunate that the journals of a number of historically significant people have survived, in particular those of John Evelyn (1620–1706) and Samuel Pepys (1633–1703). We also have the writings of Roger North (1653–1734), who was Attorney General, in which he discourses on music. He and his brother, Francis North, later Lord Guildford (1637–85), who was Lord Chief Justice and Keeper of the Great Seal to James II, were both keen amateur musicians. From these four men's records we obtain a fascinating insight into amateur music of the day and of how people from senior professional and wealthier classes evolved a firm and well-tutored interest in studying and playing music. This echoed the continuing interest of the Stuart royal court and that of William III and Mary II.

For Pepys, music was a favourite art. 'Music is the thing of the world I love most', he wrote in his diary for 30 July 1666. We are fortunate, therefore, that with his enthusiasm and his ability as a player, critic, teacher, composer and patron, he was also extremely well placed as a naval administrator who often visited ships and dockyards to observe the interests of seamen, particularly in the Royal Navy. He records many instances of the playing of music at sea, for example (23 April 1660, aboard the *Naseby*):

In the evening the first time that we had any sport among the seamen, and indeed there was extraordinary good sport after my Lord had done playing at ninepins. After that W. Howe and I went to play two trebles in the great cabin below, which my Lord hearing, after supper he called for our instruments, and played a set of Lock's, two trebles and a base, and that being done, he fell to singing of a song ... with which he played himself well, to the tune of 'The Blacksmith'.

A servant plays the tabor and drum as the steward serves dinner to Lord George Graham (1715–47) in his cabin. Oil painting by William Hogarth.

The instruments that Pepys mentions were what we call recorders. On 30 April the same year he records a different kind of instrument, which it is surprising to find on board a warship:

> After that to Poole's, a tavern in the town, [Deal] where we drank, and so to boat again, and went to the Assistance, where we were treated very civilly by the Captain [Thomas Sparling], and he did give us such music upon the harp by a fellow that he keeps on board that I never expect to hear the like again, yet he is a drunken simple fellow to look on as any I ever saw.

Naseby was the flagship of the fleet sent in the spring of 1660 to embark King Charles II after his continental exile during the Commonwealth. As soon as the King was on board, the ship was renamed *Royal Charles* and the mood of rejoicing prompted another round of music-making in the great cabin. Pepys's patron, Lord Montague himself, joined in a trio with his servant William Howe and Pepys. Howe and Pepys also played the violin, and there was an impromptu concert of what Pepys described as 'Barber's music' to celebrate the return of the King. During this they made use of 'two candelsticks with money in them for "Symballs"'.

A contemporary of Pepys, the Revd Henry Teonge, served in the *Assistance* as Chaplain. He did not like life at sea, but writes of Christmas Day 1675:

> Christmas Day we keep thus. At four in the morning our trumpeters all do flat their trumpets, and begin at our Captain's cabin, and thence to all the officers and gentlemens cabins, playing a levite at each cabin door, and bidding good morrow, wishing a Merry Christmas. After they go to their station viz. on the poop and sound three levites in honour of the morning.[61]

Roger North, who accompanied his brother on a visit to the Northern Circuit in 1676, enjoyed a special occasion afloat:

> The best entertainment he had was at Newcastle where the magistrates were sollicitous to give him all the diversion they could; and one was the going down to Tinmouth Castle in the towne barge. The equipment of the vessell was very stately, for ahead there sat a four or five drone bagpipe (the North Country organ), and a-sterne a trumpeter, and so wee merrily rowed along ... which comicall equippage afforded me infinite diversion.[62]

Music making on river and canal boats has long been a favourite amusement in Flanders and the Netherlands, as we see from charming sixteenth-century miniatures showing gentlemen and ladies singing and playing during the important May festival. A circular engraving illustrating the zodiac sign for Gemini and the month of May by de Passe gives a delightfully lively scene, the boat being decorated with boughs from trees.

On a much more dramatic occasion in 1590 when the Dutch undertook a waterborne Trojan horse initiative in order to capture the strongly fortified city of Breda from the occupying Spanish, a lone fiddler played in the boat full of turf under which the Dutch soldiers were hidden. Whether he was giving a signal to the Dutch to come out or beguiling the Spanish we do not know, but an engraving clearly shows him playing away in the bow of the boat as the soldiers quietly disembark to launch their surprise attack, which was highly successful.

About 100 years later and despite the threats of war and fighting, the playing of music and the enjoyment of open-air entertainment in boats was, if anything, even more popular, as is reflected in the publication in Amsterdam in 1654 of songbooks such as *Vreugde Stroom*, illustrated with engravings of waterborne musical entertainment and published by Jacob

Vinkel. The love of singing is also shown in an oil painting of a marine artist by J van Swieten (*c.* 1635–51), who is sitting before the easel on which his almost completed canvas stands, playing a theorbo and singing. He must have been pleased with the standard of his work!

The Matelot as a Musical Amateur

Singing played a regulation part in life aboard a Dutch warship, as we see from N Witsen's great book on shipbuilding and the organisation of routine in a crowded warship, first published in Amsterdam in 1671. He gives the words for songs which are to be sung by two seamen when turning out the watch, on the order of the quarter-master. Although the seamen were on official duty, they were amateur singers and it would be fascinating, if ear-shattering, to hear the standard of their performance and to compare this with the singing of Columbus's men at the mass in mid Atlantic.[63]

There was no comparable musical routine in an English warship, where orders were relayed by shouting or by bosun's call. However, the English love of singing and hearing music was encouraged by the opening of the first concert rooms for the recital of music to the public in 1672 by John Banister, who was followed by a coal merchant, Thomas Britton, known as 'the small-coalman', in 1678. In 1683 Mr Sadler opened his music house for concerts twice a week at the Islington Wells. Supplementing music performed in theatres and at taverns, these rooms provided venues where the public could hear classical works and popular ballads, such as those celebrating the achievements and victories of English seamen like, 'The English Seaman's Resolution' or 'The Loyal Subject's Undaunted Valour'. Another has the marvellous title, 'The Dutch Damnified; or, the Butter-boxes Bob'd'. Robinson's *Schoole of Musick* of 1603 contains 'Row Well ye Mariners', which seems to have first appeared in 1565/6. *The Dancing Master* by John Playford came out in 1650 and is an important source for unaccompanied tunes. It contains 'St Paul's Wharf', connected with taking water near St Paul's Cathedral. There is 'John Dory' of 1600, John Alldee's 'Stand Fast ye Mariners' of 1666–7, and 'Sir Walter Raleigh Sailing in the Lowlands' of 1682, still being sung in 1820.

Perhaps these lines from 'We be Three Poor Mariners', in Freeman's *Songs of Three Voices*, published in *Deuteromelia* of 1609, sum up the attitude and character of the contemporary seaman:

> We be three poor mariners
> Newly come from the seas.
> We spend our lives in jeopardy
> Whiles others live at ease.
>
> We care not for those martiall men
> That do our states disdaine;
> But we care for those Marchantmen
> Who do our states maintaine.

Such songs or more licentious versions of them would certainly have been sung at sea for entertainment.

For the late seventeenth and the eighteenth centuries more records have survived and we begin to obtain a true picture of what the ordinary seaman as well as the officers and gentry played. That fascinating independent mariner and author, William Dampier (1652–1715), records aboard the English privateer *Duke* in 1708: 'The musicians play the most popular numbers from daily life on board; tuneful lively numbers as "Hy Boys up we go"'.

At Mindanao in the Philippines on an earlier voyage in 1686, he wrote that his captain, Captain Swan, during his meals with Raja Lant had his trumpeters present: 'Captain Swan was served a little better and his two trumpeters sounded all the time that he was at dinner'. During the religious festival of Ramadan the Raja was not allowed to entertain his guests with music and dancing, but after this he amused the English captain with dances every night.[64]

By a curious twist of fate another English captain, Thomas Forrest, on an officially sponsored surveying voyage visited the same place almost 100 years later, between May 1775 and January 1776. Clearly there was a surviving tradition of music-making on both sides. Forrest took a German flute (transverse flute) with him and presented it and two violins to Raja Muda, with whom he made good friends. The Raja preferred learning by ear rather than from a score and his wife enjoyed learning songs too.[65]

Sailing in an English merchant ship of 1710, John Cremer (1700–74) records in his journal: 'The captain blowed a good trumpet, as he had two, one brass, one silver – gave grand entertainment, sung a good song'.[66]

Quiet weather and a crowded musical soirée on the stern walk of the East Indiaman Halsewell, *1786. Drawn and engraved by R Dodd.*

Aboard the Danish East Indiaman, *Jomfru Susanne*, in the Indian Ocean in November 1719:

> We had a good wind and clear weather. The Captain let the ship's folk keep themselves merry and then for every man there was drawn ½ pint Cap's [Capetown] wine and furthermore let his musicians play for the whole day.[67]

Playing music was not the prerogative of Danish and English seamen alone, as we see from the records of the Dutch East India Company and other shipping records, such as those of the Middelburg Commercial Company. Preserved amongst the latter are lists of the effects of seamen who died at sea. Traditionally, a dead man's effects are auctioned amongst his shipmates, who give generous bids, the money is then totalled and passed on to the dead man's family to help them out. Eighteenth-century records of these auctions were kept meticulously and we find that for Oberstuurman Pieter Vinck of Flushing who sailed in the *snauwschip De Vliegende Faam* of Middelburg and who drowned, he had an oboe which was sold for 4½ Flemish pounds. Similarly in Dutch naval records we find that a lieutenant owned a flute and that others had accordions, zithers, violoncellos, harmonicas and violins.[68]

In 1969 the remains of a wooden flute were found in the wreck of the Dutch East Indiaman *Amsterdam*, still held in the sands off Hastings today. From the name engraved in the wood it would appear that this instrument was made by Bernard Hemsing, a musician and instrument-maker who flourished in Leiden in 1730–40, and may have been owned by a young officer or passenger. In the tense prelude to a historic naval battle, which took place off Camperdown in October 1797, the Irish Protestant rebel Wolfe Tone was accompanying the Netherlands admiral De Winter in his flagship. While at anchor impatiently awaiting a fair wind, Tone noted: 'Admiral de Winter and I endeavour to pass away the time playing the flute, which he does very well; we have some good duets and that is some relief'.[69]

Some European voyagers noted and recorded music played by seamen from other countries. In 1751, on board the Swedish East Indiaman *Göthe Lejon*, at Whampoa, the trading settlement permitted by the Chinese, Olof Toren observed:

> It is rather interesting to watch when some officials are rowed past each other, if you like to observe the behaviour and vanity of men: Someone who goes up or down the [Pearl] river has his flag and sign by which the other recognises his station and if the man who meets him is lower in station, then he starts to beat his cong cong and then he will be answered by the same instrument. This he returns in the same way with good wishes for the journey.[70]

Seamen also noted the effect of music on wildlife at sea. On a voyage from New Guinea in 1754 the Norwegian, Johannes Rask, observed:

Porpoises always appear at sea when they hear some musical
instrument with a loud sound, which I found on the voyage
home. When our trumpeters went up on the poop and played
we usually saw them if the sea was calm and smooth and we
saw them, mostly when the sun went down almost every day
tumble round the ship in shoals.[71]

Life in a Swedish East Indiaman appeared to be more regulated. Instructions
dated 1766 for the *Louisa* on her way to Canton read:

Para 26. Also may be well those of the crew who are exercised
to a certain degree in music. They may use the violin and soft
instruments on condition that work is not neglected or some
untimely noise is made.[72]

Discipline in an eighteenth-century British Royal Navy warship was very
strict and when the ship was being handled silence was the rule, so that
shouted orders and the bosun's call could be heard and obeyed instantly.
However, in HMS *Minerva* in 1793:

On certain nights a lantern was hung up on deck and a fiddler
seated on the topsail sheet bitts, and there would be dancing
for those that cared.[73]

*Sailors dancing a final
jig in a tavern before
leaving England,
1818. Etching by
T Rowlandson.*

Discipline on warships on long voyages of exploration was usually of a slightly more relaxed nature. The relationship between officers and men, who were
usually hand picked, had to be good and could not rely entirely on official

Dance and Skylark,
1798. Mezzotint
by W Ward, after
T Stothard.

disciplinary methods when operating far from home and from Admiralty authority for long and testing periods in unknown waters and widely varying weather conditions. Almost without exception, the officers in charge saw the need for music and made certain that one or two of their men had some amateur ability. One of Captain James Cook's men, Thomas Perry, must have been in this category, for he wrote a song which has survived. One couplet goes:

We will toast Captain Cook with a loud song all round
Because that he has the South Continent found.[74]

Whilst a strong system of punishments was available to help impose order, the best ships were those in which the delicate balance of discipline was maintained by high professional standards of seamanship and leadership. That brilliant pupil of Cook and outstanding navigator, Captain William Bligh (1754–1817) who, because of his difficult personality and of the *Bounty* mutiny in 1789, must be one of the most examined naval officers in history, fully understood the value of music at sea and embarked a partially sighted Irish fiddler, Michael Byrne from Kerry, to help with relaxation and the preservation of healthy morale. Bligh insisted on his men taking exercise and dancing to maintain their good health.

Following another infamous mutiny, that aboard HMS *Hermione* in 1797 the captain's steward, John Jones, giving evidence at the court martial, said that after the act of the mutiny the mutineers called him up from below to play his flute, so that they could dance and thus relieve their feelings and preserve morale.[75]

Some Musical Explorers

Amongst the great leaders of French eighteenth-century naval expeditions exploring the Pacific, La Pérouse (1741–88), Bougainville (1729–1811) and D'Entrecasteaux (1739–93) all made sure that amongst their seamen they had some who could play an instrument. During the D'Entrecasteaux expedition of 1791–4 when they were visiting the island of Bouka in the Solomons, music was found to be extremely helpful in communicating with the island's inhabitants. 'M. de St-Aignan played quite a lively air on his violin: they seemed to enjoy the sound … which was quite novel to them.[76]

During the Freycinet expedition (1817–20) in the *Uranie*, M. Pellion wished to speak with the people of Sharks Bay, Australia, who had been very cautious about approaching:

M. Arago playing his castanets to communicate with the natives of Sharks Bay, Australia, as M. Pellion offers a gift.

I had some necklaces of glass beads which I shone in their eyes, but I could not get them to approach. M. Arago came. He approached them sounding his castanets and immediately one of the natives accompanied him by knocking a rhythm on a spar.[77]

The Spanish naval expedition of 1789–94 under Captain Malaspina was perhaps the first to investigate native cultures in the light of the teachings of the Age of Enlightenment and of Rousseau's *Dictionnaire de la Musique* (Paris 1768). It was felt that whilst the natives would have difficulty in communicating with Europeans, their culture was none the less valid and was not necessarily inferior to that of Europe. Furthermore, understanding could be gained through a form of universal exchange of the material expression of a culture, i.e. its artefacts and in particular its music, which if studied carefully, could be readily understood. Accordingly seamen and officers with musical ability were taken and written records of musical exchange with the natives were kept as an important section of the expedition's study.[78]

The men who undertook expeditions to polar regions were perhaps those who needed music most, in order to maintain their morale during the long dark hours of winter when their ships were caught in the ice or they were living in huts, separated by vast distances from their homelands. This was especially true in those periods when wireless communication and aircraft, that might bring relief, did not exist.

In the collections at the National Maritime Museum is the violin played by Rear Admiral Sir W E Parry (1790–1855) during his Arctic expeditions, 1819–27. The Scott Polar Research Institute at Cambridge has preserved in playing condition Parry's barrel organ made in London by John Longman 1801. Parry, a pioneering exponent of activities to entertain and educate his men, used to play the organ in order to get his men to march round the deck and dance when conditions prevented them going ashore for exercise. He took part enthusiastically in the elaborate fancy-dress masquerades, which were organised in the long dark hours of the Arctic winter. On one occasion on 1 November 1824, he appeared as 'a Chelsea Pensioner who had lost his right leg, playing the violin with "Sukey" his spouse playing on the tambourine'.

The banjo played by Dr L D A Hussey during the Shackleton expedition of 1914 aboard the Endurance.

Another historic instrument preserved at Greenwich is the banjo played by Dr L D A Hussey during the Shackleton expedition of 1914 aboard the *Endurance*. The banjo was the last item to be saved from the ship before she sank and proved to be a vital factor in preserving morale. It is signed by members of the expedition. On his tragic expedition to the Antarctic in 1910–13, Captain R F Scott took a gramophone and a pianola.

Scott had learned the value of having a pianola from his 1901–04 expedition in the *Discovery*, when a pianola was taken, to which he paid a glowing tribute in a letter to the manufacturers. Interestingly, Captain G S Doorly in his book about the voyage of the small steam yacht *Morning*, that went to the relief of this expedition, tells how the chief engineer and he wrote songs that commemorate the voyage and Scott's work. They also took a piano presented by Sir Clements Markham that almost did not reach the ship on time and was later threatened with destruction when insufficient space could be found for it in the ship.[79]

A Belgian naval officer who led the expedition in the *Belgica*, that was the first to spend the winter in the Antarctic in 1897–9 was acutely aware of the need for music in his ship. When the departure of the expedition was delayed, he encouraged his friend, Rahir, to form a band:

> Only ten months separate us from our departure and Coene would do me a favour by learning to play a musical instrument, for instance a cornet. The instrument will be paid for by the Belgian Antarctic Expedition Committee. Our cook, van Hemelen, who earns a lot of money, might also learn to play an instrument as well as the steward and the carpenter. This band is of great importance. It should be considered which four instruments are the most appropriate.

Alas, the intended pupils were reluctant to take up this opportunity and musical entertainment was provided by a barrel organ with paper music of the Gaviolo type made by Thibouville Lamy and Co. of Paris. This instrument was much appreciated and performed yeoman service. It is preserved in playing condition at the Nationaal Scheepvaartmuseum in Antwerp.[80]

In the British SS *Fox* sent out to find the lost Franklin expedition of 1845 to the North-West Passage, there was a more accomplished, if perhaps less harmonious orchestra which performed on New Year's Eve 1857/8 while the ship was wintering in Baffin Bay:

> At midnight the crew came in a big masquerade procession to greet the captain with full music with two flutes, one accordeon, fire tongs and frying pans.[81]

Barrel organs were taken to sea well before the late nineteenth century. The National Maritime Museum has in its collections a magnificent gilded organ that belonged to Admiral Sir Samuel Hood (1762–1814) which he took to sea and which 'served' in battle.[82] Like Parry's organ it plays a number of

The barrel organ by Broderip and Wilkinson, taken to sea by Admiral Sir Samuel Hood in the first decade of the nineteenth century.

dance tunes as well as patriotic airs. As an alternative supplement to amateur performances, which must have varied greatly in quality, musical boxes were also used. The National Maritime Museum has several that are known to have been taken to sea, but none earlier than the nineteenth century. In a Danish ship, the barque *Alexander* of Copenhagen, K E Mohl wrote:

> On 15 November 1828 we already got the Trade Winds … entering in the hot zone which we reached a couple of days later and soon greeted with thin clothes and the barrel organ.[83]

In 1912 the helmsman of the 4-masted barque *Adelaide* could not prevent himself from doing an involuntary dance to the captain's gramophone:

> The Old Man has a wonderful gramophone or whatever they call this machine and in the evening he plays to our great enjoyment. When I had a spell at the helm last night the machine suddenly began to play 'Caroline'. I was almost jumping up and down, but I contained myself with tapping my feet with a saintly smile on my face.[84]

Where proper instruments were lacking, the seaman could be amazingly inventive and ingenious, creating some astonishing 'Frou Frou' or 'Fou Fou' bands, makeshift affairs often in fancy dress. On board the 5-masted barque, the *Copenhagen*, on her first voyage between Panama and San Francisco:

> During this same motionless calm the accordeon virtuoso the sailor Guldenkrone had started an orchestra consisting of two violins, two accordeons, one drum made on board, one nozzle like a tooting horn, a triangle and a broadsaw blade, and those eight gentlemen entertained us many times with a really fascinating ensemble and a precise rhythm, which during the quiet evening hours with the moon high above proved quite sentimental. We could listen for hours.[85]

In 1862, during the American Civil War, aboard the *St Thomas* of Copenhagen:

> This evening there is life in the foc'sle. Here is a concert, song and dance. First and second violins are played quite well and one aided in a tasteful way by a triangle made of linstock, an empty tin can as drum and a children's flute on which a big, bearded man is playing in great earnest …. The melody changes into 'Yankee Doodle' and the dancers are tireless; even the slowest are drawn in.
>
> Finally the dance ends and singing begins, and you don't hear just sailor songs, but beautiful four-part patriotic songs.[86]

Song and Dance at Sea

Crews from Welsh ships were considered pre-eminent at singing; for in Wales, singing was and is, of course, a national pastime. Add to this that Welsh crews kept together over many years, moving from one vessel to another, whether Welsh-owned or otherwise. Often they came from one village or community and knew each other's families and background well. Furthermore, they had the full backing and understanding of the members of that community, who had owning shares in the ships or in the insurance, financial and chandlery businesses that maintained them. There was a very real and special kinship, especially among men from North Wales, but the whole Welsh coast bred fine seamen. Furthermore, care was taken over their education and training so that they were encouraged in their careers. Their early education was tinged with the character of their religious worship and imbued with long experience of hymn singing.

Seamen from countries other than Wales could sing well too, of course. On New Year's Eve 1917 in a Gulf port near the Mississippi:

> Suddenly from the middle of the harbour wonderful accordeon music and singing was heard, made by two Norwegian sailors who had jumped ship from the *Superior*. One played the accordeon in a strong way and the other had a wonderful voice. For about one hour they went round in a small boat playing and singing and I was touched by the music and the song in the quiet night over the mirror-calm sea, surrounded by the wooden masts from all the sailing ships.[87]

Whilst the standard of performance was not always that high, the men enjoyed singing and put a lot of gusto into it. They learned tunes from each other, and added their own words. For example, the Welsh used the tune of 'Spanish Ladies' for their song 'The Three Masted Schooner' and the tune of 'The Girl I Left Behind Me', well known in Liverpool in the time of the Crimean War when many troops were being embarked there, for 'In San Francisco Harbour'.

Some men who had a knowledge of music and had drifted into seafaring could perform well and used their time in port to take lessons. A seaman from the Revenue Cutter no. 4 in Denmark is a case in point: 'His instruments were accordeon and guitar, and as soon as the ship was in harbour he went to lessons in guitar playing.'[88]

A seaman employed by Henley Brothers, shipowners of Wapping on the River Thames in 1770–1830, who died at sea in 1812, was clearly quite a well-versed singer. Amongst other personal documentary relics which have survived, is his pocket book, in which he copied the words of his favourite songs. He had a good hand and the songs are of classic German character, rather like lieder.[89] Another seaman's pocket book with notes on songs has also survived, but this one merely serves to show how the music and words were usually retained in the memory and rarely written down because only titles and a few scrappy lines are recorded. A journal kept aboard the *Ilione* for the voyage from London to Penang and back by J Rowland is exceptional in that it contains five songs of which three have the music. A journal preserved in private hands is also exceptional, in that the writer, AB Charles H Bailey serving aboard HMS *Rover* in 1876, preserved complete songs as they were adapted aboard his ship.[90]

Rough life at sea scarcely encouraged record keeping, but fortunately towards the end of the sailing-ship era, Captain R B Whall, who had had some training in music, did record what he heard. Another person who collected songs for a much earlier period is the Norwegian, Peter Dass (1647–1707). Fortunately, through the generosity of Norsk Selskab till Skibrudnes Redning in Oslo, his work has also been published and a disc made of the music he collected.[91] Le Chasse Marée of Douarnenez in France have also done some excellent work in collecting and publishing material in recent times.

While the Welsh were pre-eminent at singing, German ships probably had the best bands. Fritz Lemmeke of the full-rigged ship *Alsterthal* of Hamburg noted in his journal of 1900:

> A German ship without music would be unthinkable in those days and we also had a small primitive orchestra. When we needed something to lift our spirits a march went round the deck to the cabin (captain's) and after a couple of pieces of music we got a bottle of some sort or another.[92]

Perhaps the captain decided to reward them in this way to stop them playing any more!

In the full-rigged ship, *Flottbek*, also of Hamburg, the band even had a crude sort of uniform:

> As traditional at that time in German sailing ships on long voyages, the crew formed an orchestra; in this case it consisted of two accordeons, one flute, a mouth organ, triangle, big drum made of a flour cask covered with sailcloth at both ends and decoratively painted; a kettle drum of a small tin can also covered with sailcoth, and castanets. Tails and tin buttons were sewn on a used jacket as a uniform for the drum major and to this was added a mace with a knob and tassles made by the carpenter. When we reached the Equator the orchestra played well together ... on the big hatch during the Dog Watch when the weather permitted.[93]

The tradition of giving special performances for feast days or any occasion the captain might approve was maintained. Usually seamen loved to dance to the music provided and were good at it. Martin Nielsen describing seafaring life in the period 1798–1816 writes of a Crossing the Line celebration in 1801:

> In the evening they started a dance which kept going the whole night. The sailors danced together with the officers and everywhere on this occasion there is a freedom and equality

... this merriment held on through three nights and days because we had good weather and a quiet sea.[94]

Of course in American ships the fourth of July was specially celebrated. A lady, Charlotte Page, records in her journal for a voyage from Mobil to Liverpool that on Independence Day 1852:

> In the evening we sent up sound rockets. The sailors got up a procession consisting of a horse, orchestra and music. The sailors had handspikes on their shoulders for guns and marched twice round the deck, after which they sang three or four songs. The Captain gave them some wine and they gave three cheers for George Washington.[95]

Some sailors were specialists in folk dancing; indeed much of their expertise must have been based on a knowledge of traditional dancing, passed on to shipboard life by men pressed into the Royal Navy or forced to go seafaring to survive. Walter Runciman of the famous British shipowning family records life in the brig *Northumberland* in 1866:

> Joseph was in great demand, as he was an expert clog dancer. He took great troubles and had much pride in teaching the younger members of the crew (which included myself) to do the various steps he best knew.[96]

A love of music and dancing was shared by seamen of all nations. Some of the finest, the Arabs who sailed dhows across the Indian Ocean, had their own tradition:

> Whenever coming into a large port that can supply the Arab sailor with the diverse entertainment that sailors of all lands expect after a long voyage, there is a great celebration. This consists of the dance so familiar among male Arabs, throughout the Arab world – dull shuffling, agitation, jumping and hopping accompanied by the loud noise of snapping fingers and moaning music from drums and tambourines. Sometimes the men are so involved that they are late in executing orders.[97]

Of the Chinese, Clausen a Danish seaman aboard the brig *Conrad* wrote in 1864: 'The Chinese seamen receive every known ship with ear-splitting music whenever she enters harbour or the roadstead.'[98]

Instruments of Choice

Many of the instruments favoured by seamen have already been mentioned. They had to be hardy enough to survive the rigours of the sea climate in all parts of the world; they had also to be fairly cheap and easy to handle in the confined spaces available. Thus in the nineteenth century a fiddle or a guitar

A sailor's tin violin made by a Redruth tin-smith, c. 1850. Legend has it that its original wooden sound-box fell apart when filled with hot rum!

were the most suitable stringed instruments. Harmonicas were popular, and for those with a little more cash to spare, flutes and maybe a trumpet were common. Squeeze boxes and accordeons are traditionally associated with seamen, but the latter were expensive and did not survive well: 'They suffered very badly from the humid air because the reeds went rusty and the bellows went out of shape. And only a few sailors could afford to buy them.[99] People often say the accordeon was invented by and for seamen, but this is not true.

In the same sort of spirit, you often hear people say that this kind of pastime died out with the end of the sailing ship. This is certainly untrue. There is, for example, the remarkable fact that a Norwegian owner who ordered a new tanker named the *Kim* to be built at Newcastle in 1930, also insisted on a good number of musical instruments being provided for the crew to play. Whilst it could not be a firm condition of employment that the men should be able to play, enough capable players were signed on for the band to play on entering and leaving harbour, and on national or public holidays or at parties, rather like a Royal Marines band. The ship was sold in 1935 when the instruments were put ashore and later presented to a town band in Bergen.[100]

A convoy escort warship of the Second World War named *Highlander* was adopted by the City of Perth and, in response to a suggestion made by one of her captains, the City gave the ship three sets of bagpipes, rather to the surprise of the crew. Considerable ingenuity had to be used to put on a public display of the men playing when the ship entered or left a Scottish harbour. The ship was definitely musical in character, the only problem being that of hoisting in the variety of instruments brought by the officers through the small wardroom hatch. They included a concert harp and a piano.[101]

An interesting study might be made of how knowledge of musical instruments was spread around the world from European origins through the influence of seamen. For example the 4-stringed ukulele often thought to be a native Hawaiian instrument is nothing of the kind. Stemming from the guitar family this instrument evolved from the original mainland Portuguese cavaquinho which survived in the islands of Madeira and the Azores as the braguinha. In 1879 men aboard the American barque *Ravenscrag*[102] brought the braguinha to Hawaii where it was reborn as the ukulele. The name means 'leaping flea' in Hawaiian.

However, music was not always welcomed aboard ship. Sailors, as has been noted, are superstitious by nature. Whistling was thought to bring a strong wind. A sailmaker of the 1900s wrote: 'At bad weather nobody dared play the harmonica. People thought it would make the weather gods angry, so that bad weather would come'.[103] A writer of 1888 reports:

> The playing of musical instruments was believed to call down a storm. At least there is many a misfortune; piano playing at the wrong moment when others want to sleep, unleashes a storm of ill will in the mess: the good harmonica in the foc'sle was usually welcome and was not reckoned among the squeaking instruments![104]

Respect mixed with superstition was shown on Holy Days as in the frigate *Bellona* off Callao in 1841:

Sir R Gordon's fancy-dress ball aboard the British frigate Blonde, c. 1860.

> On Good Friday the Catholic ships cockbill their yards and beat and drown a stuffed figure of Judas. On board the *Bellona* we commemorated the significant Holy Day by forbidding the horn blowers to blow the usual signals for meals in the mess. All drumming and music was silenced.[105]

Far from dying out the playing of music at sea is still very much alive today, though it causes fewer problems, thanks to tape and disc reproducers equipped with headphones, thus confining the sound to one pair of ears. This would have been welcome to listeners aboard the 5-masted barque *Kobenhavn* on the way from Copenhagen to Melbourne, who had reservations about the quality of the seamen's music, which sounds as if it was more enjoyable to play than to listen to:

> Our jazz band is very select. It consists of all possible and impossible instruments and a musical man, who heard it out here at sea would cross himself many times and try to get clear of this bestial noise in the easiest way. But when someone like myself is sitting in the middle of it with his accordion, conducting with my instrument, it is acceptable. Let us have the real music for ourselves with our own thoughts; then you really enjoy it! [106]

Music for Migrants

What of the entertainment of civilian travellers by sea? It is extraordinary to us to think that throughout the dangerous period of the European wars

An elegant dance on the deck of the emigrant ship Randolph *en route to New Zealand. From the* Illustrated London News, *1850.*

against Napoleon, people were still travelling on visits to countries in Europe and elsewhere, such as India and America. However, these were a minority and their travel was often connected with their professional interests in the army, colonial administration, or business. It was only some time after peace was declared that minds began to turn towards the idea of travelling in order to find improved living conditions and greater rewards in another country; migration as we call it.

In the early nineteenth century ships were mostly owned by individuals or a family. It was only when much larger sums of money were needed to finance the ships and services that companies were formed with the power to manage the complex undertakings involved. The exception to this general pattern was the East India Company, which with its Royal Charter of 1600 had an improved monopoly of trade with India until this was ended in 1883. The Company used to send groups of their ships in convoy for protection on a more or less regular basis. Many passengers were carried and the ships were well run.

William Hickey, travelling on board the East Indiaman *Plassey* in 1769 noted in his memoirs that:

> … each of the ships had an excellent band, consisting of every description of wind and martial instruments, the whole striking up the moment the sun appeared above the horison and continuing to play for an hour. The same thing was done in the evening previous to sunset, I never heard anything that pleased me more.[107]

A voyage to India could take four or even nine months, so, for the entertainment of their companions, passengers with the necessary skills would play music, some would sing and recite and others would dance. Sometimes a professional would be engaged by the passengers at their expense as we see

from an account by Frederic Fitz John Trench, who travelled on the first
voyage of the East Indiaman *Castle Huntley* in March 1826. Off the Downs
on 7 March, when some passengers were affected by the motion of the ship,
welcome distraction came from an unexpected source:

> A Punch and Judy man came on board with his paraphernalia
> and afforded us much amusement. As a means of beguiling a
> tedious hour we have engaged him to accompany us. It was
> suggested by one of the ship's officers, and no sooner proposed
> than acceded to, so little worthy of deliberation did he appear
> to think a voyage to the Eastern Hemisphere. We were able,
> with the help of his piper and fiddler, to get up some music
> and dancing for the first time, which had a very exhilarating
> effect on our whole party, everyone appearing to forget his
> bilious miseries during the day to join in the reel.[108]

So music proved a useful antidote to sea sickness, but it seems to have had a
far from therapeutic effect when a rival Danish East Indiaman, the *Jomfru
Susanne* was afflicted with an outbreak of scurvy a century earlier:

> The captain let the purser give every man half a pint of French
> brandy and then after this both his musicians had to go round
> on the deck, each with his violin followed by all the sailors in
> one long dance, and this as long as they could move. This

*An impromptu dance
below decks in a
crowded emigrant ship
bound for America.
From the* Illustrated
London News, *1850.*

should be a medicine for the same malady. but instead it enlarged the malady.[109]

There was no official provision for music by the East India Company on the long voyages to and from India, except in the case of musicians attached to Indian army regiments, who might well be expected to play. Also, as in the Royal Navy, a captain might recruit one or two musicians for his crew and pay them some extra money out of his own pocket.

As the flow of people increased, so the shipping industry, which saw an opportunity for good business, responded. In the early part of the nineteenth century passengers were usually carried as an extra to cargo, which was the prime business, and ships' accommodation was altered temporarily by erecting canvas or thin boarding partitions to meet the needs. Later, however, fast ships were designed and built specifically for passenger carrying and to transport the mails that had also increased in volume.

It was into this extraordinary, damp, heaving, risky world of brave and generous minded, but hardened seamen with their curious superstitions and special customs and music that the many migrants who travelled in nine-teenth-century ships were projected. They travelled in enormous numbers. 2,374,000 travelled from Britain to Australia and New Zealand in the peri-od 1826–1915, excluding slave or convict traffic. In an almost similar peri-od, 1820–1915, 29,218,000 people travelled from Europe generally to the USA. For the relatively brief period of their voyage, although it must have seemed an eternity at times, they had to adapt to the unsteady sailing ship world and all its appallingly uncomfortable moments. Music was a very desirable distraction.

In 1855 aboard the British passenger 'frigate' *Orwell* from London to Melbourne:

> We had thirty passengers in the tween deck amongst whom were two who played the violin, one the guitar and one the flute, and he was also a first class drummer. We soon made a very good drum out of an empty flour cask and a couple of pieces of calf skin and so we had quite a good little music band which, in the evening at 7 o'clock when the weather was good, marched in front of the passengers twice round the deck, whereafter it stopped in front of the cabin and there was dancing until 8 o'clock. When 8 bells were struck they marched once more round the deck after which the night watch was set and everybody went to his own cabin.[110]

However, another passenger, Alfred Withers, who sailed in the *James Baines*, a specially-built passenger sailing ship of the finest quality, from Liverpool to Melbourne in 1857, was not quite so enthusiastic about the musical enter-tainment provided:

> That musical treat the grand concert came off tonight in the

Ladies' Salon, there was a full attendance and all the arrangements were perfect, champagne punch, brandy ditto, wines,
oranges and co everything in proper order, but what ought to
be the cream of the thing 'O what a falling off was there my
countrymen', the vocalisation was excruciatingly bad I never
met so many with so little music in their souls ... this musical
discord is to take place twice a week on Mondays and
Thursdays which will involve the necessity of my getting up
on the shortest notice sick headache, an excuse to go on deck.

Later he wrote:

If music hath charms to sooth the savage breast ours has the
contrary effect on the breast of sickness, for many in the middle
of the concert were seized with qualmishness. 'Sick? On no,
only rather queer', and retired with anything but soothed
countenances to their various cabins, it may be that the comic
songs were too much for the ladies for from the inmost recesses
of their cabins came noises, which resembled in some degree
hysterics, a noise as if they were completely frustrated and
worn out with the labour of laughing.[111]

Music in the Age of Steam

The advent of steam power eventually brought greater speed and reliability,
and as iron and steel became used for building ships it became possible to
build to far greater capacity and higher safety standards. At about this point,
owners conceived the idea of running liners, ships that would travel on certain lines, i.e. between given ports, Liverpool to New York, say, at regular
times, rather like maritime buses. This kind of service which had to be regulated by international agreement, lasted until the advent of mass air travel
after the Second World War.

With the coming of company operation of sail and steamships, and competition for the increasing number of passengers, owners began to provide
musical entertainment instead of relying on the passengers to make their
own. At first this usually took the form of providing a piano or perhaps some
fiddles for passengers to play, but the famous Black Ball Line took a particular advertising line, by providing bands on their larger ships. There were usually five players, who also doubled as stewards. Evening dances were held on
the poop deck, but this was not always an easy matter. As M Stammers
records in his book, *The Passage Makers*, a passenger, Mr Hopkins, travelling
in November 1855 noted in his diary:

The scene was a very gay one; we found it very difficult to
dance as the poop was on one side so much and the vessel
going at a great rate, but it added to the fun of the evening.

In cold weather the passengers danced frequently to keep warm. As the larger

Three ladies play their guitars aboard an excursion steamer. Engraving by G Cruickshank.

steamships began to dominate business, companies provided professional musicians to entertain, usually whilst passengers took a morning relaxation or their afternoon tea. In the evening, music would be played during dinner and/or for dancing afterwards.

As early as 1841, just four years after the foundation of P&O, we find the Managing Director writing to the Purser of the newly built 1700-ton *Oriental*, destined for the run to Alexandria:

> I wish you could pick up three or four musical fellows such as they have on board the *Liverpool*; nothing contributes more to harmony (in every sense) on board than a good band.[112]

And in the P&O records held at the National Maritime Museum at Greenwich, there is a letter of 1859 which suggests that everything was done to the sound of music in at least some ships of the fleet:

There is a band aboard Benares and everything in her is sounded with a bugle instead of the usual bell.[113]

Failing the provision of music by members of the ship's company, or in addition to it, passengers would regularly organise musical entertainments of their own, no doubt of variable quality. In a little book called *Ship-bored* published in 1924, Julian Street advises seafaring passengers: 'If you ever decide to end it all, there is one humane suggestion I would make. End it all before the ship's concert'.

Here's an account of one such event during the days when P&O provided the bridge to India:

> On Tuesday evening a grand concert was given by the passengers of the Second Saloon. The night was warm so the piano was taken on deck. Mr Rooney opened with a violin selection, then Mr Pountney rendered 'My Sweetheart when a Boy' and Miss Vivian 'The Daily Question'. My Whittaker followed with a recitation capitally rendered, 'In the Engine Shed'. That fine song 'The Mighty Deep' was rendered by Mr Hosking; Miss Davis played 'Dans le Bois' as a piano selection and Dr Smith's burly voice rolled out 'Father O'Flynn'. Four little maids then concluded the first part by 'I don't want to play in your yard'. After a brief interval Mr Hosking sang 'Simon the Cellarer'. A recitation, 'The Elf Child' by little Miss May Longmore was followed by 'The Death of Nelson' by Mr Whittaker, who had to respond to an imperative encore.

The quaintly attired group in this photograph, taken c.1912, call themselves a 'fou fou' band, adopting a sailor's slang term for the perfumed talcum powder formerly issued to treat prickly heat.

The operatic company en route to Egypt entertain the Prince of Wales in 1875. Note the milk supply and standard of accommodation. From the Illustrated London News.

In his book *The Only Way to Cross* about the great transatlantic liners, John Maxtone-Graham tells us that ships' concerts of this kind had largely fallen out of fashion before the First World War, but he quotes the programme of a second -class concert on Cunard's *Aquitania* in 1921 which sounds remarkably similar to the one outlined above. It was chaired by a certain Revd Roberts and included songs, a piano solo, a dance, 'highland buffoonery', comic patter and concluded with 'Miss Isabel Brown's celebrated whistling solo'. One notes that both these entertainments were given by second-class passengers: presumably those in first class would have thought such things beneath their dignity.

In providing music for their passengers the directors of ocean-going ships were actually some twenty years behind those who operated coastal, canal and river services. These locations had seen the earliest application of steam power in ships. Together with transport it seems to have been normal to provide musical entertainment, certainly on the Thames and canals in southern England where the weather was more reasonable. A few convivial songs no doubt added greatly to the joys of an outing on the water.

The massive increase in the number of passengers travelling by sea, especially on transatlantic, but also on Far Eastern routes, can be readily seen from the increase in size of ships built to carry them. Brunel's *Great Britain* of 1843 was some 3,618 tons; the *Oceanic* of 1871, 3,708 tons; the *City of Paris* of 1888, 10,500 tons; the *Mauretania* of 1906, 31,938 tons; the *Queen Mary* of 1934, 80,774 tons and the *Queen Elizabeth* of 1938, 83,673 tons. Large companies were established to finance and manage the extensive business of building and operating such ships and of providing for the numbers of passengers carried. Whilst many emigrants travelled cheaply in fairly basic conditions, passengers paying full fares

could travel in a very luxurious state and the owning companies felt the need to ensure that they were suitably entertained by providing music, which would have been played by live musicians during mealtimes, at leisure time concerts and recitals, as well as for dancing in the evening. Many well-known and popular musicians and bands were employed or established their reputation in this way.

International classical artists were treated with great respect and might or might not consent to perform. This was in marked contrast to the opera company who travelled in the P&O ship *Sumatra* from Brindisi to Egypt in November 1875, in order to entertain the Prince of Wales and the Viceroy of

Detail from the replica of the memorial erected in Southampton to the musicians of the ill-fated SS Titanic.

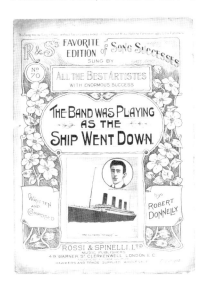

The music publishing business was not slow to cash in on the Titanic disaster. These are just two of the songs it inspired, c.1912.

Egypt in Cairo. Their conditions and the condescending attitude of 'the aristocracy of the saloon and cabins' were thought worthy of comment in the *Illustrated London News* of the day.

The most admired of all sea-going musicians were surely those aboard the ill-fated *Titanic*, who played heroically until the angle of heel of the deck of the sinking ship rendered this impossible. The evidence for what they played is contradictory, which is scarcely surprising in the circumstances of this tragic night in 1912, but witnesses agreed that the musicians played to the last possible moment. A monument was erected as a tribute to their gallantry in Southampton.

On several occasions in the period between the First and Second World Wars, bands of the British armed forces took passage in passenger liners to undertake overseas concert and ceremonial engagements. One military musician, F J Ricketts, better known as 'Kenneth J Alford', the famous composer of military music, was particularly involved in this way. In 1925, as the Bandmaster of the Argyll and Sutherland Highlanders he journeyed with his band to New Zealand in the New Zealand Shipping Company's vessel *Rotorua* and in the following year returned to the UK in the same company's ship *Remuera*. Again in 1939 when, as the Director of Music of the Royal Marines Plymouth Division Band, Ricketts took passage with his band to Canada in the Canadian Pacific liner, RMS *Empress of Australia* and, after the outbreak of war in September 1939, returned to England in the CPR ship *Duchess of Richmond*.

On each of the voyages, these two military bands presented daily concerts for the benefit of their fellow passengers who, on each occasion showed their appreciation to the musicians by presenting each of them with a suitable memento, whilst Major Ricketts was the recipient of an inscribed ceremonial baton. Among the many marches composed by him as Kenneth Alford are, 'On the Quarter Deck', 'The Middy' and 'By Land and Sea'; he was also the arranger of the Royal Marines regimental march, 'A Life on the Ocean Wave'.

After the Second World War owners continued to build large passenger carrying ships such as the *Empress of Canada* for Canadian Pacific, *Windsor Castle* for Union Castle, and *Canberra*, all of which were launched or entered service in 1960. However, by comparison with aircraft, such ships were desperately uneconomical to run. In 1950 ships carried three times as many passengers as aircraft, but by 1965 were carrying scarcely any. The jet-engined aircraft had taken over and the days of the great liners and the musical entertainment provided aboard were past, although some of the ships continued to ply successfully in the holiday cruise trade.

Today there is a great demand for cruising holidays on the part of those who seek relaxation and a small measure of adventure aboard comfortable ships. Many rival companies seek to meet the demand in a highly competitive market, though at the time of writing, a number of major companies operate as subsidiaries of a single organisation – the massive Carnival Cruise Lines of the USA.

P&O claims to have invented pleasure cruises as long ago as 1844, when the company gave a free ticket for a Mediterranean voyage to the famous novelist W M Thackeray. He published an extensive journal about the trip under the pseudonym Michael Angelo Titmarsh. This turned out to be good

publicity for P&O. Although he was critical of some of his shore excursions, Thackeray was happy with the experience as a whole. He described it as 'so easy, so charming, and I think so profitable, that I cannot but recommend all persons who have time and means to make a similar journey'.

Nowadays, some cruise passengers love to exhibit their own talents in karaoke evenings in one or other of the ship's bars, and sometimes, if time allows, a chorus of passengers is formed to rehearse under expert guidance and take part in a concert performance of a well-known work

The supreme elegance of the first-class lounge aboard the Winchester Castle, *c. 1930.*

such as Handel's *Messiah* or a Gilbert and Sullivan opera. But in general music on cruises is provided by professionals. A large ship will carry its own show company, several star entertainers and more than one band. Sometimes a specialised team of classical musicians will be engaged to extend the range of the music on offer. Even with fully functioning stabilisers, the motion of a ship at sea is not always helpful to musicians, and it pays to make sure the grand piano is very firmly anchored to the floor.

Thus the seafaring minstrel continues to earn his keep in the twenty-first century, much as he did in days long past.

Whilst it is slightly beyond the scope of the present work, let us also remember that the skippers, boat men and women who worked the barges on inland waterways also had their musical traditions. They played and sang their own songs, particularly the river folk of the great European rivers. Dr Charles Burney (1726–1814), the British musicologist, noticed their singing in his voyage by raft on the Danube to Vienna from 24–30 August 1772.[114]

There were also the boat people of the great American rivers, such as the Missouri and Mississippi.

Turning to the amateur sailor who has his own boat, the yachtsman, we find that he enjoys making music at sea just as much as his professional counterpart. Usually this is on an accordion or other easily stowed instrument, but a wealthy owner can afford to have a piano fitted into his large yacht. One French owner, Le Baron de l'Espée, had his boat designed and built around his piano.

The grandest yachts were the royal or imperial yachts, an expression of the power and majesty of their owners and their nations. These could embark a marine band that would play to entertain guests or would accompany special ceremonial. The Royal Marine band of the former British Royal Yacht *Britannia* played a most important part in her ambassadorial role around the world notably with their 'beating retreat' ceremonies, as well as providing much entertainment for the Royal Family and their guests on board.

OPPOSITE Musical box from the wardroom of HMS Canopus, launched in 1897.

5 Shanties and Traditional Sea Songs

When as our Ships with merchandise are safely come to shore,
No men like us under the skies to drink, to sing, and rore...

John Playford, The Jovial Mariner

The most common maladies amongst the crew of a sailing ship were those associated with overstrained muscles such as torn ligaments, slipped discs and hernias, not scurvy or malaria as many people imagine. This is because the whole operation of controlling a sailing vessel depended on human braun, or 'Armstrong's Patent' as it was nicknamed. Hoisting or changing a heavy canvas sail, rigging a top gallant mast, adjusting the yards and sails when changing course, pumping out water from the bottom of the ship, all had to be done by men heaving, hauling or pulling. Yes, there were pulley blocks to lighten the load and capstans and windlasses could give a degree of help; but all still depended on the minds and muscles of men. In the second half of the nineteenth century, which marked the beginning of the end of the sailing-ship era, improved forms of windlass, capstan and pump were devised and, of course, steam power in the shape of a small auxiliary engine, the donkey engine, was gradually fitted in ships, providing a mechanical power source that could be applied to lighten, if not replace the human effort required.

We get some idea of what all this meant, what tremendous demands it put on men who were already having to cope with pounding seas, a bucking ship and poor food, when we visit a preserved ship such as the *Cutty Sark* in Greenwich, or HMS *Victory* in Portsmouth. Looking up at the complex array of ropes, heavy yards and heavier masts we wonder how on earth the seamen managed. We share something of their experience if we go sailing in a yacht, but the gear and sails today are ultra lightweight; after all, this sort of sailing is meant to be as relaxing and pleasurable as possible. Nowadays it is very difficult for us to gain any real idea of what it was all like. We have so many machines, fork-lift trucks, special forms of winch, grabs, dumpers, lifts and hoists, many governed by remote control and operated at the lightest touch of the electronic button, that we just do not have to make the same physical or mental effort. Such, however, was the life of the seaman and it was all the harder when owners scrimped and saved on food and reduced the size of crews in order to make maximum profit from their ships.

The men's muscle power was most efficiently used when they all pulled or heaved together and at precisely the same moment. To help achieve this, music in the shape of the 'shanty' was and still can be invaluable. The origin of the name shanty for a seagoing work song is still debated. It may derive from the French *chanter*, to sing, or it may relate to the heavy labour involved

in removing Caribbean beach shacks, or 'shanties', in the hurricane season. Even seamen smugglers in the eastern maritime Pyrénées had a special shanty to assist with the heavy work of heaving their contraband over this mountainous region to the Catalan coast. The shanty system worked extremely well, because the singing also kept the men amused and therefore happier. Their minds and hearts as well as their muscles were well occupied and coordinated. A shantyman who could lead this kind of chorus with humour and precision was a great asset to a crew. His talents were literally worth those of several men put together. Consequently, good shantymen were much prized by skippers and owners.

A fiddler playing on the capstan of the 4-masted barque Medway, *1912, as the men work the capstan.*

The original shanties would be quite unrecognisable to most of us today. They were like crude, rhyming sounds roared out with the barest gesture to music in a regulated, rhythmical chorus. The words were often, but not always, coarse in content. What did this matter? The men and ship were hundreds of miles from delicate society and ears. The important business was to get the job done as rapidly and efficiently as possible. The shanty and the language were seamen's special aids. If a sensitive lurking soul happened to overhear and did not like the tone of it, then that was their misfortune. This was the seaman's special equivalent of 'music while you work'.

Whilst it would be quite false to put them into rigid categories, one can give shanties rough groupings according to the nature and rhythm of the tasks they supported. Weighing anchor with the capstan could take a long time, most of a day in difficult circumstances with a heavy ship. Although the work might go fairly easily and rapidly while the slack in the cable was being taken in, it would soon become slow and heavy as the ship came up to her anchor, the cable tightened and men pushed with all their strength

ABOVE *Clewing up the mainsail in stormy weather. Painting by A Briscoe.*

RIGHT AND OPPOSITE *Heavy hauling set to music, 1886.*

HAND OVER HAND.

on the chest-high capstan bars in order to hold the heavy ship and prise the anchor from the sea bottom. Thus a shanty with a slow tempo, plenty of verses and choruses would be used. Tradition has it that where a suitable fiddler was present he would sit on the capstan and play. This was occasionally true, although it probably only occurred in warships, smart Indiamen or the later packet ships. Typical shanties for this work are 'Shenandoah' or 'Homeward Bound'.

Windlass work was jerkier in character because the men pulled the operating levers up and down in a shorter rhythm. Usually the accompanying shanties were four lines long. Pumping shanties used when pumping ship, with a similar up and down movement on the handles of the old pumps, were of a like kind. 'Strike the Bell' is an interesting example. The Downton pump was introduced later and was operated by 'bell' ropes attached to the handles or cranks on the large wheels, which turned the axles of the pumping mechanism. The wheels turned fairly rapidly and with a flowing rhythm, which suited all kinds of song, so no particular sort was needed. 'A Rovin' is a typical pumping or capstan song.

Hoisting a tops'l or t'gallant, the sails nearer the top of the masts, means hauling on the ropes called halyards (haulyards); a longish task but with a shorter paced rhythm. The hauling part of the rope falling down from above would be rove through a special block fixed to the deck and so out horizontally along the deck. The men would then line up behind each other facing the shantyman who, with the bosun or one of the mates, would be hauling on the vertical falling part of the rope. The shan-

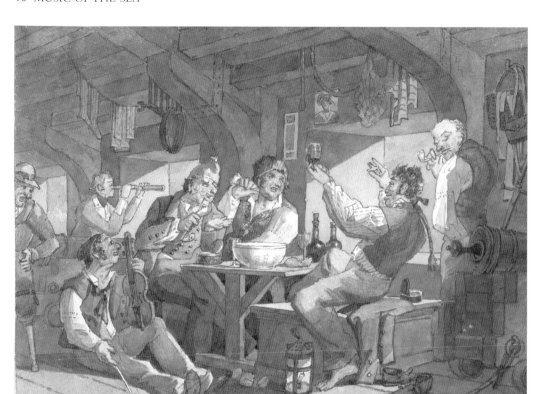

Shipmates carousing. Watercolour by W H Pyne, c. 1804.

tyman would sing out and the others would respond. 'Blow the Man Down', 'Reuben Ranzo' and 'John's Gone to Hilo' are typical hauling shanties. 'Whiskey Johnny' is another that was used for pumping and various tasks.

An alternative method for this kind of hauling was to 'Stamp "n" go'. Here the men turned their backs to the fall and the shantyman, and stamped with their feet to keep the rhythm going as they hauled on the rope. Normally this kind of hauling was practised only in ships with large crews. A famous shanty for this is what we call 'Drunken Sailor' today, but which had an older title 'Early in the Morning'. Tradition has it that the latter shanty was used in ships of the East India Company and was also permitted in certain warships of the Royal Navy. This was exceptional and probably refers to smaller ships, because the normal rule was silence, so that the orders or bosun's call could clearly be heard and discipline maintained over a large body of men at tricky moments when sailing or in battle.

On many occasions a short haul only was needed in order to hoist smaller and, therefore, lighter sails or to 'sweat up', i.e. to make the final tightening haul in order to get a good set on a sail. For these, two line shanties with a quick rhythm were used such as 'Boney', 'Hanging Johnny' or 'Johnny Boker'. Where the short haul was hand over hand, i.e. literally two or three men pulling with one hand after the other, special phrases or lines with emphasised syllables or shouts were used. These might be unintelligible, obscene or nonsensical but had a good rhythm to suit the work.

There was also what was called a 'sing out', which was a form of basic chant used to initiate a haul or some other operation. The form of this was very much the private creation of the shantyman and could be quite original, as long as it served the purpose of encouraging the men to work hard and pull together at the right moment.

If leisure time was allowed, and this depended on having consistently good weather with a fair wind, it would normally be in the first or second dog watch, between 4.00 and 6.00 p.m. or 6.00 and 8.00 p.m. This was usually the case in the trade winds which blew steadily in the same direction allowing a moment for relaxation, instead of the restless activity involved in constantly changing the arrangement of the sails to catch a fickle wind or put the ship about. Singing was a favourite leisure activity and seamen knew many songs, which are often given the classification of 'forebitters', because the men tended to cluster around the forebitts, double bollards used for making the ship fast when alongside and such things. On the eighteenth-century wooden warship the bitts were heavy wooden structures like a crossbar. Here, those interested would gather round with the fiddler or squeezebox player and sing away at such songs as 'Spanish Ladies', 'Maggie May', 'Liverpool Judies', 'Cawsand Bay' or 'Dundee Whalers'.

Music of the Whalers

Whaling ships had their own songs and French, German or Dutch ships might have a different watch-keeping system, whereby there was a long afternoon watch from 12.00 to 6.30 p.m., which introduced an opportunity for variation in singing traditions.

Saturday night at sea in a British warship, c. 1800. Etching by G Cruikshank for Dibdin's Sea Songs *of 1841.*

SATURDAY NIGHT AT SEA.

RIGHT AND OPPOSITE Countless versions of Britain's nautical anthem have appeared since Thomas Arne wrote it for the masque Alfred *in 1742.*

RULE BRITANNIA,

NATIONAL SONG AND CHORUS,

NEWLY ARRANGED EXPRESSLY FOR THIS WORK.

ENT. STAT. HALL. THE MUSICAL TREASURY. PRICE THREEPENCE.

55

PUBLISHED AT PETER'S HILL, NEAR ST. PAUL'S.

Amongst the toughest of whaling men were those who manned the American whalers sailing out of ports such as Nantucket in the early days, then New Bedford, Sag Harbour, Fairhaven, Mystic and many other New England and Atlantic coast ports. A whaling voyage could last up to four years, during which time the ship would sail from Arctic to Antarctic waters across the Atlantic and Pacific Oceans. The conditions in which the men lived, especially during a polar winter period, scarcely need description. Despite this, and the deprivations caused by wars with the British and by the American Civil War, the American whaling fleet was active well into the nineteenth century.

Their music has some particularly interesting characteristics: songs such as 'Clear the Track' show elements of African influences. These were picked up when the men sang their songs in the ports of the Deep South, such as New Orleans, and were heard by the African stevedores and others who made their own adaptations which were later passed back to visiting seamen from

RULE BRITANNIA.

A Celebrated National Air Composed by Dr. Arne.
Dublin. Printed and Sold at Rhames's, Nº 16, Exchange Street.

When Britain first at Heav'n's command,

rose from out the Azure Main, arose arose from out the Azure Main.

This was the Charter, the Charter of the Land, and Guardian Angels

sung this strain, Rule Britannia, Britannia rule the Waves, Britons never will be Slaves.

2
The Nations (not so blest as thee)
Must in their turns to Tyrants fall,
While thou shalt flourish great and free,
The dread and envy of them all.
Rule &c.
3
Still more Majestic shalt thou rise,
More dreadful from each foreign stroke,
As the loud blast that tears the Skies,
Serves but to root thy native Oak.
Rule &c.

4
Thee haughty Tyrants neer shall tame,
All their attempts to bend thee down,
Will but arouse thy gen'rous flame,
But work their woe and thy renown.
Rule &c.
5
To thee belongs the rural reign,
Thy Cities shall with Commerce shine,
All thine shall be the subject Main,
And ev'ry Shore it circles thine.
Rule &c.

6
The Muses still with Freedom found,
Shall to thy happy Coasts repair,
Blest Isle, with matchless Beauty crown'd,
And manly hearts to guard the Fair.
Rule &c.

American and European ships. Other songs such as 'Rolling Down to Old Maui' tell of the men's uproarious activities in Maui, an Hawaiian island where the whalers called after a hard season in northern waters or elsewhere. It typifies their feelings at being back in warmer tropical climes.

Whaling men sailed from many countries, but the ships and achievements of the Americans are recorded with great pride and flair in museums in the old whaling ports, such as New Bedford, Nantucket and Mystic, as well as at Kendal. One should also remember the men of the Down Easters, the great East Coast trading schooners, such as were built at Bath, Maine; of the famous Blue Nose fishing schooners out of Gloucester; and of the early American trading vessels from Salem, all of which are commemorated in local museums.

Whilst there were certain national characteristics in leisure songs, which could be quite marked, for example in Welsh manned ships, they were in general very international in character. They belonged to the world of the

Dance music, published c. 1855, named after HMS Agamemnon, the first warship designed as a single-screw battleship. She helped lay the first transatlantic cable in 1858.

THE
AGAMEMNON QUADRILLES

Introducing the following popular airs

JOLLY YOUNG WATERMAN,
BAY OF BISCAY, POOR JACK,
TWA'S IN THE GOOD SHIP ROVER,
THE SIGNAL TO ENGAGE,
HEARTS OF OAK,
COME MY LADS THE BATTLE'S O'ER,
RULE BRITANNIA,
AND
GOD SAVE THE QUEEN
COMPOSED & DEDICATED TO
REAR ADMIRAL
SIR EDMUND LYONS
BY
HENRY OAKEY.

LONDON H TOLKIEN PIANOFORTE MAKER 27 28 & 29 KING WILLIAM S.T. LONDON BRIDGE

sailor man, who might come from any country and who would borrow a tune and put his own words to it or who might make up his own tune. There was no idea of copyright, although as mentioned, you might reasonably expect a Scandinavian seaman to produce a different kind of song from a Frenchman or a Spaniard.

The favourite tunes were common currency and, although adapted to suit the singers' nationality and native tongue, were instantly recognisable. For example 'A Rovin'' was frequently adapted. It might start: 'In Amsterdam there lived a Maid', or 'In Plymouth Town there ...'. Amsterdam might be a tavern not a place and the sailor might go to Chile or elsewhere before returning home. In 'Liverpool Judies', which is about men being shanghaied by crimps and brothel keepers, usually after landing in New York, the words could be altered to tell the story from a different port. Normally the seamen's additions or variations were obscene and licentious.

Here's something to keep the small-boat sailor on his toes! Published c. 1850.

Who Created the Nautical Ballad?

Argument rages about the difference between sea songs as sung by sailors at sea and ballads or songs about the sea sung on land. There are differences, but one should not be too dogmatic about this, because ballads were written by seamen as well as landsmen, and sailors would sing both when at leisure. The choice was theirs and as long as they knew the words and a tune, they would sing what they liked.

Clearly some ballads were written by landsmen rather in the way of news reports and were quickly hawked around the streets of a city in order to gain a profit for the author and publisher. Very often a fresh tune was neither written nor published, but a suitable existing one would be suggested. This was a form of folklore inheritance from the town crier or even the waits and minstrels, by means of which the author and publisher hoped to make a financial profit. Should his song be taken up and sung in

Just one of the many songs that celebrate the virtues of an idealised Jack Tar, published c. 1902.

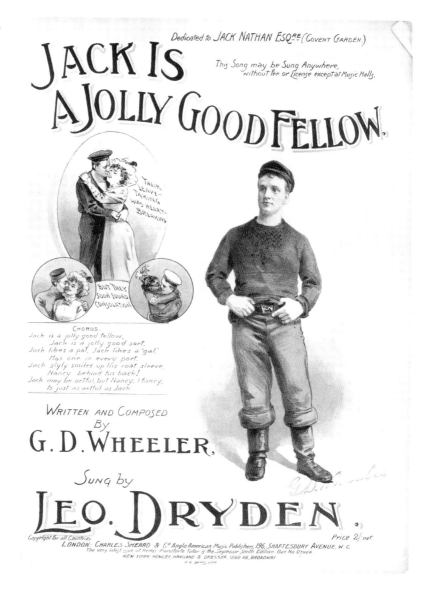

the taverns then he might do well. One thinks of the example of a ballad recalling George Clifford, 3rd Earl of Cumberland, and 13th Lord of Skipton Castle, which was written in commemoration of his part in the Armada fighting in 1588, and was still being sung in the cottages in Skipton in 1920![115]

Some ballads were made up and printed from very old oral sources, especially when printing became cheaper and easier, and publishers were looking for material that might sell well because of popular interest. Should such a song become accepted amongst sailors, knowledge of it would be spread overseas and perhaps a new market created. London, as the biggest port city in Britain, was the main market, but Liverpool rivalled it when trade, particularly the North American, West Indian and the emigrant and general passenger business developed. Other seaports and even land-based cities such as Birmingham had publishers of ballads, who included songs of the sea in their stock. The sea was

THE PILOT'S DAUGHTER JANE.

SONG.

POETRY BY J. E. CARPENTER,

THE MUSIC COMPOSED BY

FRANZ ABT.

LONDON. ROBERT COCKS & Cº NEW BURLINGTON STREET, REGENT STREET, W.

The German composer Franz Abt (1819–85) lends his talent to yet another nautical tear-jerker, c. 1866.

a popular topic, partly because Britain's trade success depended on shipping and partly because seamen had become a familiar folk subject.

Production of ballads increased greatly during periods of war when dramatic fights, battles and escapes formed appealing topics. However, the subjects for ballads were not confined to wartime dramas alone. These merely provided the extra 'spice'. In peacetime, storms, shipwrecks, cannibalism and rescue, partings and the stresses of life, all formed subjects for songs. In an age when the majority of people, and particularly seamen, could not read, the oral and sung tradition was a potent means of expression and communication. There was a big market too. Recent research has indicated that between 1580 and 1780 the number of seamen rose proportionately four times faster than that of the population of England and Wales. The total for 1780 has been estimated at 111,000.

Most writers of ballads and sea songs were aiming at this market, including those in the top flight such as Thomas Arne (1710–1778), the composer of 'Rule, Britannia!', first heard in 1740 in the masque *Alfred* and Charles Dibdin (1745–1814). 'Rule, Britannia!' is an absolute show-stopping British piece, but in the case of Dibdin some of his best tunes have a universally appealing beauty. A good example is 'Tom Bowling', which he wrote in commemoration of his brother, Captain Thomas Dibdin, but which is also a mark of respect for the character of the seaman which stirred a deep note of affection in British hearts. Thus at the top end of the creative source and the market there were men who could achieve attractive heights of composition. There were also amateurs such as Thomas Gray, Assistant Secretary of the Marine Department, Board of Trade, who wrote 'The Song of the Life Boat's Crew' to be sung to 'Heart of Oak', which was published in 1869.

Over the Sea to Skye

In a very special class is the music of the fishermen and people who in every sense lived by the sea in the Hebrides, the Western Isles of Scotland. Some of the men sailed deep sea in large fishing vessels or other ships, but the majority were coastal fishermen with a particular cultural background strongly influenced by firmly held religious beliefs of the Calvinist persuasion. However, in reality their home culture was steeped in a very much richer musical tradition distilled over centuries from a blend of Celtic and widespread European origins, brought by seamen, some marauders and some traders, and preserved orally by singing and by mouth music, a kind of articulated humming, practised by a people who did not have easy access to instruments for financial and geographical reasons. This distillation produced some of the most beautiful songs about the sea and sea life. The names of the composers are lost in the mists of time. Many of the songs are very old, having traversed the shoals of the ages through the natural skills of the performers who were untrained except in the school of their homestead, where their teachers had themselves been taught by their elders. There is an amusing record of one lady from whom music was collected around 1905 who had learned from another old lady, whose mother remembered Dr Johnson's visit in 1773 and him drinking eighteen cups of tea for breakfast!

On the same visit to the Western Isles Dr Johnson and his travelling companion, James Boswell, heard something of this music. Dr Johnson noted:

> They accompany in the Highlands every action, which can be done in equal time, with an appropriate strain, which has, they say, not much meaning; but its effects are regularity and cheerfulness. The ancient proceleusmatick song, by which the rower of gallies were animated, may be supposed to have been of this kind. There is now an oar-song used by the Hebrideans.[116]

Fortunately, the Hebridean songs were collected and preserved by Marjory Kennedy-Fraser (1857–1930) and Kenneth Macleod in the

1900–30 period, whilst they were still very much part of the daily life of the island people. Although performance of the original mouth music was already beginning to disappear, Marjory Kennedy-Fraser describes hearing some:

> This mouth music for dancing is characteristic and exhilarating in the extreme ... the electrifying effect of which I shall never forget ... I can quite believe, as old people have assured me, that this voice music had a passionate quality exceeding that of any dance music produced by instruments.[117]

The songs were created for and by island communities, who had to work hard by land and sea to survive, but who had the ear and inclination for music. Many of them were sung as an accompaniment to work and are exceptionally fine examples of shanties. Others are lyrical and descriptive, movingly expressive of the life of people whose daily routine is intermingled with the sea and fishing. Marjory Kennedy-Fraser describes how she had to scramble to collect some of the seamen's songs, a hazard being the set of the tide and the fishermen's need to make the best of any decent weather. On one occasion she wanted to collect a song from a fisherman who was mending nets aboard his boat in the harbour and who would set sail at noon. The only way of reaching him was by water and she invoked help from the highly respected local priest, who gave orders for her to be taken out in a small boat to meet the man who:

> Was busy with his nets, and they chaffed him, I could see, about the strange lady who was running after him for his singing. So I had to wait about half an hour before he would be persuaded to sing although the men urged him with 'Suas leis an oran'. He continued mending his brown nets in the glorious morning sunlight, with the purple sea lying quiet round us. But at last he yielded and having once begun sang verse after verse, and I got it noted down. He sang it with a peculiar woodwind like quality of voice, which suggested a theme for orchestral treatment.[118]

Some songs are an ultimate expression of sea life such as 'Seagull of the Land under the Waves', 'Sea Sorrow', and the 'Skye Fisher's Song', which is the one Mrs Kennedy-Fraser collected with such difficulty. Others are working songs, such as the rowing song, 'Sea Sounds' and the shanty 'The Ship that Saileth Home'. Born of the sea they express its movement, life and colour, plus its mystical and tragic quality.

The Story of the Shanty
The oldest recorded form of nautical working song must surely be the ancient Egyptian fishermen's chant of about 2,500 BC, which they sang as

they drew their nets in, hoping for a good catch: 'It comes and brings us a fine catch.'[119] Then there are the chants used by the oarsmen in the Greek triremes. Whilst these were, as far as we know, just chants, not songs, they performed the same function, encouraging the men and getting them to pull together. As has been mentioned, the Vikings also had rowing chants which must have been used during the period of their maritime strength in AD 650–1050. References to later medieval working songs are virtually non-existent but we know of yelps and shouts used by seamen when setting sail and raising anchor given in the St James of Compostela pilgrim ballad of the fifteenth century, a working habit that must already have been very old.

There are other references in the fifteenth century, including some to the seamen on the Spanish and Portuguese voyages of discovery, but the first recorded actual words for European working chants are given in the *Complaynt of Scotland* published in 1549.[120] They include a bowline call, hauling and anchor calls, which appear to have a Norman/Flemish linguistic origin and which were preserved by the Scottish seamen. There is a curious dearth of knowledge of English shanties of the seventeenth and early eighteenth centuries. Why this should be is difficult to understand. Perhaps they were taken for granted and their language was so obscene as to be 'beyond the pale' for people to record. This is our loss. Even Shakespeare does not mention such a kind of song. In contrast and as already mentioned, there are many, many songs about ships, seamen, pirates, battles and the like in English and other languages. Amongst the English songs of this period is 'John Dory', which seems to have been well known in the mid sixteenth century. It tells of the defeat of a French privateer by a Cornish captain, John Dory, and has a strong patriotic character that made it a favourite.[121]

Interestingly, one of the earliest seventeenth-century references to working songs is given by William Dampier on his voyages to the Far East where he notices the natives singing as they work on their boats in about 1690. Thomas Forrest sailing in this area in 1776 mentions the same. Fortunately, he recorded his experience and the music as best he could:

> The Moors, in what is called country ships in East India, have also their chearing songs; at work in hoisting, or in their boats a rowing. The Javans and Molucca people have theirs. Those of the Malays are drawling and insipid. In Europe the French provençals have their song: it is the reverse of lively. The Mangaio is brisk, the Malabar tender.[122]

A hundred years later Miss L A Smith in her book *Music of the Waters* (London 1888) mentions boatmen's songs from India and what is now Pakistan or Bangladesh. They are mostly rowing songs from men working on the great Indian rivers, Ganges, Brahmaputra and Indus, but there are also songs from the boatmen who ferried cargoes ashore from the large ships anchored off shore. The lack of harbour facilities meant that in many places, especially Madras on the east coast of India, the only way to unload was to hoist out the cargo by small amounts into boats waiting alongside, which would then be rowed ashore through the heavy surf. This required skill, good timing and maximum effort from the rowers, who would be helped and encouraged by a rousing chant. On the western Karnatic coast the fishermen and others had similar chants which are still in use today and which fortunately have been the subject of a study directed by Professor K Bhat of the Nalanda Regional Resources Centre at Udupi, who has recorded them. The boatmen off the west coast of Africa at Accra performed a similar task and also had chants, but these have not as yet been recorded. In the Pacific Ocean the New Zealand Maoris and the Tahitians are famous for their boating songs. Recent versions of these have been influenced by European modes, but are still very attractive. Some dilution has occurred to suit the tourist industry, but at least this has ensured preservation of elements of the originals.

All this indicates how music in the shape of a working song or chant is by no means of Western origin. In fact the Eastern and Indian are probably of much older date. Research has also shown that just as the European-based shanties were influenced by American and other working songs, so the Eastern and Indian varieties were influenced by melodies from other sources such as Persia and the Arabian Gulf. It will take a great deal more research before one can begin to trace the exact national elements involved and how these came to be adapted and absorbed, and when, but a blend did take place and can be recognised by those who are knowledgeable. In Eastern music with its different harmonies, scales and rhythms this is a complicated study to try, but could be very rewarding. It would also reveal more of the seaman's character and social habits, and possibly indicate general patterns of trade routes.

American Influences

Important contributions to the international repertoire of seamen's songs and shanties came from Celtic countries such as Brittany and mainland Scotland, from northern Europe, Scandinavia and Mediterranean countries, in fact from all over the world, and not least from North America. Here, as noted, there was a turbulent mixture of musical influences from many European nations and in particular from the African population, who had been brought across the Atlantic as slaves. Theirs was a life of great hardships, which only eased sometime after the end of the Civil War and the abolition of slavery in 1865. Unable to buy instruments they improvised them, particularly stringed ones like the guitar. Their African, especially West African, musical tradition with its emphasis on complex rhythms and antiphonal singing seemed to have survived generations of captivity and led them to create an interpretation of working songs that had considerable influence. Performance was started by a leader, then all who wished joined in, maybe an octave higher or lower and using words that were sounds rather than meaningful. It was an act of brilliant extemporisation which maintained a marked rhythm and helped with working movements. Because Afro-Americans were present in large numbers, especially in the Southern States, their music became widespread, not least on the rivers and in the ports where they were employed as cheap labour. After the Civil War and freedom from slavery they were shipped as crew in coastal and deep sea sailing vessels. There were also those who worked as lumbermen, supplementing the large number of men and different forms of music in this business.

It would be difficult to quantify and evaluate the influence of their homespun music, but it certainly spread far and wide and was extremely popular. Many fine examples of shanty and song resulted. 'Shenandoah', named after a celebrated Indian chief, is the best-known example, but 'Rolling Home', has something of the same character. 'Lowlands' is a good example of a cotton port song and 'Blow Boys Blow' is of African origin.[123] The Civil War in America also gave birth to a number of marching songs that were converted into sea songs; the two mainly used in this way being 'Maryland' and 'Dixie', the latter being the favourite.

Earlier the discovery of gold in California and the consequent Gold Rush of 1849 had brought an instant demand for many more and faster ships to transport prospectors from the East Coast and New York to the West, the sea route round Cape Horn being quicker and, to our surprise perhaps, safer than trying to cross the plains and mountains of the continent, which were largely unexplored and fiercely defended by native Americans. This sudden, dramatic situation and the many stories of the miners caused an explosion of new songs, of which 'Banks of Sacramento', better known as 'Camptown Races', is a good example; another is 'Clear de Track, Let de Bulgine Run'.

Because of its African origins and because it was relatively cheap and easy to make out of scraps of material the favourite instrument was the 5-string banjo. This could be strummed solo or in chorus giving rise to the 'minstrel' style and band which became a fashionable favourite in many countries after the 1850s. Examples of this kind of instrument are known to have been made at sea. A fine one made entirely out of whale bone was acquired recently by the Kendall Whaling Museum in 1988.[124] This kind of work is usually classed as scrimshaw and was a favourite spare time occupation amongst seamen, whaling men particularly, of course. Sticks, ornaments, recorders, domestic utensils were all made out of whale bone and beautifully ornamented with fanciful engraving.

In Europe and the Americas shanties died out as true working songs with the end of the age of sailing ships. Powered ships can follow their course with minimum human effort. Three men can do the work of thirty much of the time. No need to call out a tired watch to perform almost superhuman feats in a dangerous storm or to drive tired men to trim the sails for the umpteenth time in order to make the best of a changing wind. Consequently there is no need for a shanty to encourage or a song to amuse in the dogwatch.

Shanties are sung, of course, but as an amusement by amateur sailors, yachtsmen, members of naval clubs, or mad museum people and preservationists. Not that their enterprises should be scorned, however, for they are preserving a precious heritage and with increased leisure time more people are taking a careful interest both in studying and maintaining the actual vessels, where they still exist, and the way of life and music that went with them. At the annual sail training races, wooden boat shows and gatherings such as that held at Greenwich and at Douarnenez in France, where Le Chasse Marée do such good work, the organisers are beginning to give prizes for the most musical crew, and recordings of the old music are sold.

Among the tangible forms of the music that commemorates ships and seamen are the attractively designed covers for songs and for dances of the late nineteenth and early twentieth century, such as the quadrille. These often express the real feeling people had for the seaman and his life. It is good that they have been preserved as some evidence of a former age whose spirit is now well gone and was mourned as short a while ago as 1931 by David Bone who had tasted the old days, but was then a wireless operator. He commented thus on a nautical ditty he heard on the air:

> The singer had a splendidly robust baritone voice, exactly the hail of a lusty son of Esau on the out-board end of a capstan bar. He sang 'Rio' with fine flourish: his chorus of four or five voices did their best.

> A fine song! But it was no chanty [sic]. I listened in vain for the rhythmic stresses of labouring men, each bearing manfully his weight on the task. The breathing moments of the song had no stir, as of a working movement. It was all wrong.

> No. He had not got it right; he had the air, but nothing of the spirit. I came out of the wireless cabin thinking of changed days at sea, and of occasions when I had heard that 'Rio Grande' chanty in real deep-water session.[125]

6 Soothing Airs

This music crept by me upon the waters,
Allaying both their fury,
and my passion,
With its sweet air.

William Shakespeare, The Tempest

S ir John Theophilus Lee officially joined the Royal Navy at the age of five-and-a-half and having gained two years' seniority, went to sea and to war aboard HMS *Barfleur* in 1795 at the age of seven. After the initial excitements of being aboard a warship amidst a large convoy of merchant ships, sea sickness and other concerns set in. As a very young midshipman and son of the first lieutenant, he was allowed to live with the other officers in the wardroom and he recalls his first evening there, when he was not feeling at all well:

> The lights now being brought into the wardroom, some officers amused themselves by playing billiards on the rudderhead, while others sat down to a rubber of whist, all enjoying themselves one way or another, till bed time, – the soft tones of a flute, played by one of the officers soothed all into harmony, and made him [Lee] quite forget his malady in the joyous feelings to which it gave rise.[126]

The therapeutic effect of music was appreciated by both officers and men, as is indicated by the case of a ship's fiddler, James Martin, who was serving in another famous ship, HMS *Queen Charlotte,* in 1795–7. Martin had applied for his discharge on the grounds of ill-health, which puzzled the Admiralty, who did not want to lose precious manpower and so, despite Martin's lowly rank, asked the Fleet Captain, Sir Roger Curtis, for an explanation. The latter consulted the captain and reported:

> Having consulted with Sir Andrew Douglas thereupon, I find that the reason of his not doing Duty, is not from ill-health as he sets forth, but from his being excused the Common Duties of the Ship that he might contribute to the Amusement and consequent Health of the Ship's Company by playing the Fiddle to them; and Sir Andrew and I are of opinion his being Discharged would be injurious to the Ship, inasmuch as it would deprive the People of a principal source of their cheerfulness and merriment.[127]

In view of this report the Admiralty did not approve the discharge!

The court martial proceedings that followed a more dangerous happening, the mutiny aboard HMS *Hermione* in 1797, reveal that the mutineers felt the need for music to relieve the stress engendered by their action. In his evidence the captain's steward, John Jones, stated that after the mutiny he was called up from down below by the mutineers to play his flute, so that the seamen might dance and thus gain relief for their feelings through the therapeutic effects of music and dancing.[128]

Therapy is close to morale boosting and the value of military and naval music for fighting men was well known, as can be seen from the following graphic statement from Wynken de Worde published in 1582 in Bartholomew's *De Propietatibus rerum*:

> Also in bataylle the noyse of the trompe comfortyth werryours
> and the more stronge that the trompynge is the more stronge
> and bolde men ben to fyghte: and comforthyth Shypmen to
> suffre alle the dyseases and travelle.

Music and Medicine at Sea

The surgeons who served at sea in the sixteenth century would have been quite familiar with the idea of music as therapy, which was passed on to them from the medical men and philosophers of ancient times. Plato, Aristotle, Celsus and Arctus all applied it. Democritus used the flute in an attempt to fight the plague; Galen recommended it for those bitten by vipers and Cato and Theophrastes used it to reduce pain. Homer believed it could reduce haemorrhage. Jean Baptiste Porta throught that diseases could be cured by flute playing, so long as the flute used was made from a tree or bush specific to the disease concerned. Paracelcus considered flute playing would cure epilepsy, without appreciating it might also cause this affliction. As Quintillian wrote, 'Give me knowledge of the principles of music, which have the power to excite or assuage the emotions of mankind'.[129]

Put in simple terms, the Renaissance medical mind felt that man should have an equilibrium with nature and that the health of the natural world was

A flautist amid the bustle of the midshipman's berth aboard a British warship, c. 1830. Note also the fiddle-player with his music book and pet monkey! Painting by Augustus Earle.

held in a balance related to the four elements, which in turn were related to the four humours, four temperaments and four musical modes. The playing of related music would have a healing effect on a patient.[130]

In his great two-volume book on the history of music published in 1776, Sir John Hawkins tells of the common use of the cittern in barbers' shops, where minor operations were performed, as well as hair cutting and tooth extracting. This was a cheaper form of lute, straight rather than round-backed, something like a modern guitar, and it was available for customers to play before attendance by the barber. It became the symbol of prostitutes as well as barber surgeons. Hawkins mentions how in Ben Johnson's *Silent Woman*, a man takes a wife on the barber's recommendation, but finds she is scarcely silent: 'That cursed barber, I have married his cittern'. The instrument was hardly ever silent in a barber's shop. Hawkins explained:

> In Morley's time, [i.e. the sixteenth century] and for many years after, a lute or viol, was part of the furniture of a barber's shop which was used then to be frequented by persons above the ordinary level of the people, who resorted to the barber either for the cure of wounds, or to undergo some chirurgical operations or, as it was then called, to be trimmed, a word that signified either shaving or cutting and curling the hair; these, together with the letting of blood, were the ancient occupations of the barber surgeon.[131]

Living as we do in an age when the two professions are very distinctly different, it may be a little difficult for us to understand the old relationship between surgeons and barber surgeons. Surgeons were usually university trained and were highly skilled, very often holding the dual qualification in both surgery and physic, which was the responsibility of the most senior medical practitioners, the physicians. Barber surgeons practised surgery after a seven- or nine-year apprenticeship to a master surgeon, after which they had to qualify by examination. Barbers confined themselves to their own profession, although sometimes carried out minor surgical duties as well.

Henry VIII had shown a great interest in medical matters and sought to reform the whole system partly because he recognised the need to provide qualified surgeons for his army and navy. Thus, by the time of the *Mary Rose* (*c*. 1512–45) surgeons in the fleet were being carefully selected. This was the responsibility of the Barber-Surgeons' Company, which had been founded by an Act of 1540 uniting the former Fellowship of Surgeons with the Barbers

Shawm, in two parts, recovered from the wreck of the Mary Rose, *sunk in 1545.*

Company. It was on this basis that in 1588 the surgeon general, William Clowes, appointed experienced surgeons to serve in the ships of the English fleet that fought against the Spanish Armada.[132] Hence, barber surgeons occupied a special place in the musical and cultural life of their time. Called upon to serve at sea, they brought with them their music, so it is scarcely surprising that a shawm was found at the door of the surgeon's cabin in the wreck of the *Mary Rose*. This was a commonly used instrument, an ancestor of the oboe, which could well have been used for therapeutic purposes.

Why Music is Good for Mariners

Whether the eighteenth-century naval officers who insisted on retaining the services of James Martin to play his fiddle in the *Queen Charlotte* ever read any contemporary medical treatises we do not know, but had they read R Browne's, *Medicina Musica* or a *Mechanical Essay on the Effects of Singing, Musick and Dancing on Human Bodies*, published in London in 1729, they would have found their views fully supported. In a work that has surprising sympathy with more up-to-date studies he writes:

> If Singing, as I have before abundantly proved, has such an Influence over the Minds of Man as to raise it to a degree of Mirth and Joyfulness … there is then a plentiful and regular Secretion of Spirits and if the Motion of the Heart and consequently the Circulation of the Blood depends upon the Influx of Spirits, Singing then must certainly be the cause of a full and strong Contraction of the Heart; whereby we may suppose that the Blood will be thrown out with a force sufficient to conquer all the Resistances it may meet with in its Passage through the Body.

Similarly Captain William Bligh, and others, would have been pleased with Browne's words on dancing:

> My Design is here to shew, that Dancing, take one case with another, though an Exercise scarce ever applied to the Cure of Diseases is nevertheless not inferior to any whatever, provided it be used with Discretion.

Eighteenth-century naval officers had some sound ideas for maintaining good health on board their ships.

A definite official move was taken to link music with health in the Danish Royal Navy of 1805, as we see from the Admiral and Commissioner's letter to the Master of Stores at the Navy Yard, in which he gives an order that the pupils of the School of Music should also be taught to be barbers; 'So that on board ship they could do the service of the barbers as well as the trumpeter'.[133] However, this move may have been dictated by financial stringencies rather than care for seamen's health!

A French nineteenth-century admiral of Huguenot descent, Jauréguiberry, who went on to be a Minister for the Navy in the French Government,

1879–83, perhaps because he was able to overwhelm his adversaries in debate with his loud naval voice, nearly lost his position in his defence of music for his seamen. In a struggle with his rival, Jules Ferry, he insisted on French warships and shore bases being supplied officially with mechanical pianos. This proposal raised the temperature and pace of a ministerial debate very considerably, but Jauréguiberry stuck to his point and, in the end, won. The mechanical pianos were supplied, much to the pleasure of the men.[134]

Among a series of articles published in the *Nautical Magazine* of 1833 and entitled, 'A Sailor's Advice to his Son on entering the Royal Navy', a senior officer includes one on the subject of music. The style is pompous and over-elaborated, but in the meat of the article the father gives strong general support to the views held by Jauréguiberry and other naval officers. He writes:

> The mariners of those vessels which navigate the Mediterranean Sea always sing in concert with the guitar, and, although to our rough tars it may seem to be an effeminate occupation, it is nevertheless a better pursuit than the roaring of bacchanalian intoxication, accompanied with black eyes. On a still evening when calm, clear and unruffled the azure transparence of the sea glows beneath the milder beams of a retiring sun; when every light and lofty sail just sleeps in its concave form, and silently the prow divides the rippling water, to take a station in some retired part of the upper deck, and leaning over the ponderous rows of artillery beneath, to hear among the surrounding vessels the plaintive chorus rise from some unseen little barque, awakens a train of reflections too elevating to be reprehensible.[135]

The reviewer of the article, writing in the 1833 edition of *Harmonicon*, applauds these words, particularly because, coming from an unexpected profession, they show a real appreciation of the therapeutic quality of music. Recognising that seamen cannot be expected to reach the highest standards of sophisticated performance, the reviewer nevertheless allows a special place for their contribution:

> In its simplest from music requires neither skill nor precautionary steps to find access to the heart, the ploughboy's carol, the milkmaid's ballad, the seaman's ditty or the recitation of the foreign mountaineer chanted with inartificial melody, produce powerful and pleasing sensations.[136]

Recent, clinical research has made progress in investigating the effects that music has on the mind and so the body, which Browne and a later writer, Brocklesby, in his *Reflections on Ancient and Modern Musick with the Application to the Cure of Diseases*, published in 1749, explained as best they could. Brocklesby sums up the problem in his day thus:

> To explain by what hidden means and secret springs of action the mind comes to have any influence upon matter is,

I apprehend, a problem too difficult to be solved upon our present principles of knowledge.

Investigations have, within the limits of available techniques, measured the autonomic response, i.e. the response of the nervous system to musical stimulus. It has been shown that this will depend on the state of the person's general health, age, sex and lifestyle, including background education, all of which condition the autonomic regulatory processes. The attitude of the patient to the piece of music concerned will also be important. Standard of reproduction must be very high and volume suitably adjusted so that there is no cause for an antipathetic reaction. The kind of response, whether it is respiratory, affecting breathing; circulatory affecting the heart and blood system or motor, which induces activity, will depend on the person's autonomic response and the kind of music played. A lively march or dance will normally induce a motor response which goes to the legs and so encourages a dance movement. Attempts by the patient to constrain movement reactions will be very much limited.

Respiratory changes can be quite marked and vary from one person to another. Circulatory reaction can be conditioned by the level of volume and by the rhythm of the music. A slowing of rhythm will probably produce a slower pulse rate and vice versa. However, it is the emotional element in the music which is the most powerful stimulant and there will be a marked difference in effect on a performer and a listener. The person who has the greatest emotional affinity with the music will react the most strongly.[137]

An experiment involving the late Herbert von Karajan, who was an enthusiastic yachtsman, measured his pulse rate whilst conducting a certain piece of music. The results showed that his rate was doubled at moments where he was most involved emotionally. These were not moments of the greatest physical activity but when, as he himself recognised afterwards, the music had the greatest emotional impact, which could come with the anticipation of some great surge in the score. The increase in pulse rate was markedly greater than that provoked by the operation of landing his private aircraft, which it might be thought would be a time of far greater tension. Measurements have also been made of other people's muscular activity and response, when listening to different kinds of music whilst carrying out a variety of activities such as dancing or working out a problem on paper. The results indicate how different personalities vary in their reaction.[138]

From these clinically controlled observations, the practitioner can advise on the use of music as an aid to maintaining good health amongst seafarers in the constrained environment of ships. This could be particularly valuable on modern warships, where the crew spend much of their time in an enclosed environment, operating technological aids rather than handling equipment on an open deck, which is likely to be a more healthy activity. Experiments are being carried out on this and on the value of music in helping the injured to recover after battle or mishap. At the time of the Falkland Islands conflict, the commanding officer of the Royal Marines band found that the spirits of the wounded were greatly uplifted when his musicians played during their transit from shore to ship and ship to hospital treatment. Thus the ancient understanding of the value of music in therapy is borne out by modern clinical research.

7 Music Born of the Sea

There is a rapture on the lonely shore,
There is society where none intrudes,
By the deep sea, and music in its roar...

Lord Byron: Childe Harolde

Although seafarers have, for a long time, resorted to music as an aid to hard labour and as a means of relaxation, and although the seaman's character has long been celebrated in song, the sea itself has not, until relatively recent times, been regarded as a source of musical inspiration. Maybe the majority of people thought of the sea as just a vast monotonous waste, and shared the view of life at sea so tellingly expressed by Dr Johnson. 'No man will be a sailor', he wrote, 'who has contrivance enough to get himself into a jail; for being in a ship is like being in jail with the chance of being drowned … a man in a jail has more room, better food, and commonly better company'.

Johnson was writing in the middle of the eighteenth century. Soon the Romantic movement would view the sea in a different light. For musicians as for painters and poets, the sea became a symbol of everything that was grand and wild and untamable in nature, an eternal challenge to man which is at once terrifying and seductive.

Before the nineteenth century there was very little music about the sea. The famous *Water Music* by George Frederick Handel (1685–1759) was put together for one or more royal evening parties on the River Thames, the best documented being a trip from Whitehall to Chelsea and back on 17 July 1717, when King George I was accompanied in the royal barge by his mistress and her husband, who paid for the expedition. The Prussian Resident in London described the arrangements as follows:

> Next to the King's barge was that of the musicians, about fifty in number, who played on all kinds of instruments, to wit trumpets, horns, hautboys, bassoons, German flutes, French flutes, violins and basses; but there were no singers. The music had been composed specially by the famous Handel, a native of Halle and His Majesty's principal Court Composer. His Majesty approved of it so greatly that he caused it to be repeated three times in all, although each performance lasted an hour, namely twice before and once after supper. The [weather in the] evening was all that could be desired for the festivity, the number of barges and boats filled with people desirous of hearing was beyond counting.[139]

Handel's *Water Music*, as it's most often performed today, consists of three suites of short pieces, none of which has anything to do with the sound or movement of water, though among the dance rhythms represented is the 'Hornpipe' which in the eighteenth century had become popular with sailors.

Handel's German contemporary Georg Philipp Telemann (1681–1767) also produced a suite of Water Music. It was written for a celebration to mark the centenary in 1723 of the College of Admiralty in Hamburg, the seaport city which exployed Telemann as its Director of Music for nearly fifty years. The form of Telemann's Water Music, entitled *Hamburger Ebb und Flut* (Hamburg's Ebb and Flow) is that of a French Overture or Suite. As in Handel's *Water Music*, many of the movements are dances, but Telemann gave them titles which link them to mythological creatures of the sea. Thus we encounter Neptune in Love, the Jovial Triton, the Turbulent Aeolus (god of the winds) and the Amiable Zephir along the characters represented, and the suite ends with a lively *canarie* entitled 'The Merry Mariners'.

HMS Vanguard, *a third rate of 74 guns, was Nelson's flagship at the Battle of the Nile (1798). His sensational victory inspired a great deal of music. This is taken from* Emma, Lady Hamilton's Songs, *published in c. 1810.*

At about the same time as Handel and Telemann were producing their Water Music, the Italian Antonio Vivaldi (1678–1741) composed a descriptive violin concerto with the title *La Tempesta di Mare* (The Storm at Sea). It was published in the set of concertos Op.8 known as *Il Cimento dell' Armonia e dell' Inventione* (The Test of Harmony and Invention), which also includes the famous 'Four Seasons' concertos. These contain imitations of natural sounds such as bird song which were not that rare in Baroque music, particularly of French origin, but for a composer to create a musical picture of the sea at that period was quite exceptional.

When the eighteenth century was nearly over, one of its greatest musical masters, Joseph Haydn (1732–1809), produced a Mass which acquired maritime associations. Originally entitled *Missa in Angustiis* (Mass in Dangerous Times), it

THE SAILOR'S FAREWELL.

Farewell! Mary, I must leave thee,
  The anchor's weighed— I must aboard,
Do not let my absence grieve thee,
  Of sorrow do not breathe a word :
What though the foaming ocean sever
  Me from thee, yet still my heart
Loves you, Mary, and will ever,
  Though stern duty bids us part.

Farwell! Mary, dearest Mary,
  Do not grieve, I shall return
Crown'd with laurels, pray do smother,
  That sad sigh, oh! do not mourn,
You unman me with your kindness,
  Oh! chase these tears off my brow,
Now round thy lips sweet smiles are creeping.
  Bless thee, Mary, farewell now.

Farewell! Mary, do not weep so.
  Though I leave thee for awhile,
I'll love thee still when on the deep now,
  Cheer my heart with thy sweet smile,
Soothe my parents with thy kindness.
  And I'll bless thee when far away,
Oh! forgive my youthful blindness
  For I can no longer stay.

Dearest parents, farewell kindly,
  Rest content whilst I'm away,
Mark that gun, 'tis to remind me,
  On shore I can no longer stay ;
The anchor's weigh'd, the sails are spreading,
  The boat is waiting in the bay,
Farewell now all kind relations,
  Pray for me when far away.

[14]

THE ROVER OF THE SEAS

I'm rover of the seas,
  And chief of a daring band,
Who obey all my decrees,
  And laugh at the laws of the land.
Wherever my swift bark steers,
  Desolation and rapine are spread,
And the names of the famed buccaneers
  Fill the bosoms of all with dread.
          For I'm Rover of the Seas—
              Ha ! ha !
          For I'm Rover of the Seas.

King of the waves am I,
  And rule with despotic sway,
As over the waves I fly,
  In search of my lawless prey.
No mercy I ever show
  To any I chance to meet—
But 'neath the billows they go,
  For dead men no tales repeat.

I'm the terror of the main,
  For none yet has conquered me,
And every victory I gain
  Makes me firmer the lord of the sea;
In storm, or in calm or in fight,
  I ever am the same,
And dearly have earn'd the right
  To claim my blood-stain'd name.

I envy no king on shore,
  For there's none has power like me,
They're bound by the oath they swore
  While I am reckless and free ;
And tho' danger I meet each day,
  Yet merry my life is pass'd
For let there come what may
  I can but die at last.

WALKER, PRINTER, DURHAM.

Two of the innumerable ballads inspired by the seafaring life. Taken from Naval Songs: Broadsheets, *c. 1780.*

was being rehearsed at the Esterhazy Palace of Eisenstadt on 23 September 1798 when news reached Haydn of Nelson's brilliant victory over Napoleon's fleet at the Battle of the Nile; and the story got around that Haydn added trumpet fanfares to the Benedictus movement in honour of this momentous event. The story was untrue, for trumpets at this point in a mass setting were conventional, as a salute to the Messiah, 'who cometh in the name of the Lord'. But the

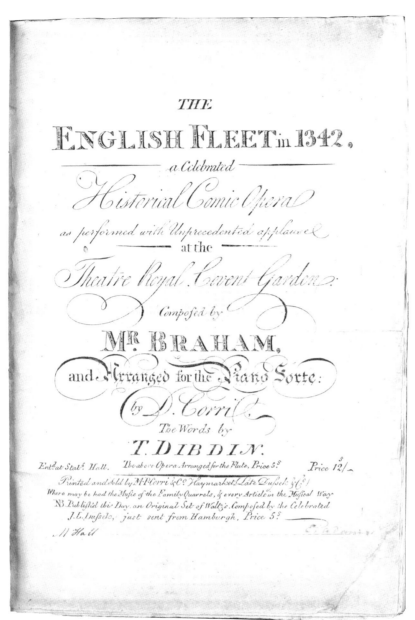

THE

ENGLISH FLEET in 1342,

a Celebrated

Historical Comic Opera

as performed with Unprecedented applause

at the

Theatre Royal, Covent Garden

Composed by

MR BRAHAM,

and Arranged for the Piano Forte:

by D. Corri

The Words by

T. DIBDIN.

Ent.d at Stat.s Hall.   The above Opera Arranged for the Flute, Price 5.s   Price 12/-

Printed and Sold by Mr. Corri & Co. Haymarket, Late Dussek &c.
Where may be had the Music of the Family Quarrels, & every Article in the Musical Way.
NB Publish'd this Day, an Original Set of Waltz's Composed by the Celebrated
J.L. Dussek, just sent from Hamburgh, Price 5.s

The composer of this rousing, patriotic piece sang at Admiral Lord Nelson's funeral. Performed during the Napoleonic War, it celebrates an English victory during the Hundred Years War, and perfectly illustrates maritime influence on shore-based creativity.

Mass did become directly linked with Nelson when the great Admiral stayed at Eisenstadt for four days during his overland journey from Italy to England in September 1800. The Mass was probably performed in Nelson's honour on that occasion, and has ever since been known as the 'Nelson Mass'.[140]

The Sea and the Symphony Orchestra

Beethoven was the first of a series of great composers who, in the nineteenth century, extended the expressive range of the orchestra and learned how to make ever more effective use of this rich palette of instrumental colour. With these resources at their disposal, composers were able to attempt portraits in sound of the sea in all its awesome variety.

THE ENGLISH FLEET IN 1342.

Illustration from the title page of the Historical Comic Opera, The English Fleet in 1342, *c. 1803.*

Richard Wagner.

Among the earliest nineteenth-century masters of the orchestra was Carl Maria von Weber (1786–1826). His opera *Oberon* includes the aria 'Ocean, Thou Mighty Monster', whose surging theme dominates the splendid overture to the opera.

Whether Nelson enjoyed that performance at Eisenstadt is open to question. It seems Britain's greatest naval hero had little or no feeling for music; indeed he once told his wife he positively disliked it. As a young captain in the Caribbean, he criticised his Commander-in-Chief for playing the fiddle. 'As his time is taken up tuning that instrument', he wrote, 'you will confidently expect the squadron is cursedly out of tune'. Later he ungraciously described Italy as 'a country of fiddlers and poets, whores and scoundrels' – which doesn't put musicians (or poets) in very good company.

Nelson's story, however, inspired music of many kinds. The Battle of the Nile, and especially the catastrophic explosion that destroyed the French flagship *L'Orient*, inspired a spate of piano fantasias and poems of which the most famous example is 'The Boy Stood on the Burning Deck' by Mrs Felicia Hemans. A new verse was even added to the National Anthem, beginning:

> Join we great Nelson's name
> First on the roll of fame,
> Him let us sing …

We know that Lady Hamilton, who had a powerful soprano voice, sang it in Nelson's presence at a dinner in Prague to celebrate his birthday on 29 September 1800, and history records no objection on the Admiral's part to that musical performance. After Nelson's death, the actor and singer John Braham was prompted to write a dramatic ballad called 'The Death of Nelson'. Some time after Trafalgar, the bereaved Emma, perhaps unwisely, went to hear Braham sing it, and distraught sobs were heard from her box.

But it's another overture we think of as inaugurating the link between the symphony orchestra and the sea. In 1829 the young Felix Mendelssohn (1809–47) visited Scotland, a country which, for an educated German of that period, represented everything that was most Romantic. On a rough day in August, Mendelssohn went on a boat trip to the island of Staffa in the inner Hebrides where the amazing rock columns of Fingal's Cave made a deep impression on him. In a letter home, he wrote: 'In order to make you understand how extraordinarily the Hebrides affected me, the following came into my mind there'[141] after which the young composer scribbled a few notes of music which become the main theme of his overture *The Hebrides* (Fingal's Cave). The overture has been regarded as the equivalent in music of the seascapes of Turner in painting, foreshadowing the work of the Impressionists. Richard Wagner regarded *The Hebrides* as Mendelssohn's masterpiece, and Brahms said he would gladly give all he had written to have composed this overture.

Felix Mendelssohn.

The Hebrides was not Mendelssohn's only sea piece. He first saw the sea on a family holiday in 1824 and was inspired by the experience to begin planning an overture which took its title from two poems by Goethe: *Meeresstille und Glückliche Fahrt* (Calm Sea and Prosperous Voyage). Goethe was delighted: 'Sail well in your music', he wrote to the young composer, 'and may your voyages always be as prosperous as this one'. Both Mendelssohn's sea overtures went through many revisions before they reached the concert platform. *The Hebrides* was first performed in 1832 and *Calm Sea and Prosperous Voyage* a year later.

In the summer of 1839, Richard Wagner (1813–83), together with his wife, Minna, and their pet Newfoundland dog, Robber, set sail in the schooner *Thetis* from the Baltic city of Riga bound for London. The voyage should have taken eight days but what followed was a three-and-a-half week nightmare at sea. The ship was subjected to a series of terrifying storms, and at one point the captain was forced to take refuge in a Norwegian fjord, where the Wagners landed briefly at the fishing village of Sandvika. This would become the setting of the first act of Wagner's opera *The Flying Dutchman*, first seen in 1843. But it was the stormy seas which had brought the story to Wagner's mind – the legend of the Dutch sea captain condemned for blasphemy to sail his ship for ever unless redeemed by the love of a faithful woman. Wagner wrote: 'I saw the whole story of the Flying Dutchman filled with the roar of the sea, which took such complete possession of me that it cried out for artistic reproduction.'[142] The sea also plays a major role in Wagner's *Tristan und Isolde*: the first act is set on board a ship bound from Ireland to Cornwall in the middle ages.

With the music dramas of Richard Wagner, the Romantic impulse of the nineteenth century was at full flood, with its passionate interest in human emotions and the mysterious depths from which they arise. In this context

Franz Joseph Haydn.   many artists in all media were drawn to the sea, as volatile as human nature, now violent, now calm, an unplumbed world of incessant movement and ever-changing colour.

Symphonic Seafarers

There's a small group of composers who had professional experience of the sea. Prominent among them is the Russian Nicolai Rimsky-Korsakov (1844–1908) who showed early aptitude for music but was entered by his father in the Marine Academy of St Petersburg. There followed two years and eight months as a midshipman in the clipper *Almaz*, but music was not forgotten. The talented lad maintained a correspondence with the father-figure of Russian romantic music, Mily Balakirev (1837–1910) and, while the ship was undergoing a refit on the River Thames, he composed part of his first symphony. Eventually the *Almaz* returned to Kronstadt near St Petersburg, and Rimsky was able to enjoy direct contact with Balakirev and his circle of gifted musicians. Eventually the budding composer landed a job in the navy, which was to some extent congenial: he was made Inspector of Naval Bands. Sounds of the sea are heard in two of Rimsky-Korsakov's orchestral works: the 'Musical Picture' *Sadko*, which tells of a Novgorod minstrel summoned to play for the underwater subjects of the Sea King; and the Symphonic Suite *Sheherazade*, which begins with the tale of the sea and Sinbad's ship; in the final movement the sea thunders through the orchestra, driving a ship to disaster on a magnetic rock. It was Balakirev who suggested the idea of *Sadko* to Rimsky-Korsakov. Balakirev had been very impressed by the so-called 'Ocean' Symphony composed in 1851 by the Russian pianist-composer Anton Rubinstein, and he thought that a nautical subject would also be suitable for a musically gifted naval officer.

Nicolai Rimsky-Korsakov.

A small digression while we're on the subject of music from Russia. In the mid twentieth century, the Armenian composer Aram Khachaturian (1903–78) produced a piece of music which for British ears is strongly evocative of the sea, though originally it had nothing whatever to do with salt water. This is the Adagio of Spartacus and Phrygia, a romantic pas de deux from Khachaturian's 1956 ballet *Spartacus*, which proved a perfect choice as the theme tune of the British TV series about a Victorian shipping dynasty, 'The Onedin Line'.

A composer who was nearly sent to sea as a boy was the great Frenchman Claude Debussy (1862–1918). In a letter addressed to his publisher, Durand, the composer said: 'You perhaps do not know that I was destined for the fine life of a sailor and that it was only by chance that I was led away from it. But I still have a great passion for the sea'.[143] Debussy was telling Durand about the three 'symphonic sketches' which make up *La Mer*, completed in March 1905. This is one of the finest of all musical portraits of the sea in all its natural grandeur, and it's slightly odd that Debussy should have chosen to relax for a month that summer in the stuffy respectability of the Grand Hotel at Eastbourne, described by the composer in a letter to a friend as 'a little English seaside place, silly as these places sometimes are'. *La Mer* was first performed in Paris in October 1905, prompting a torrent of hostile reviews. Debussy's interest in the sea as a subject accorded with his view of what music should be: 'A free art, a spontaneous open-air art, an art commensurate with the elements – wind, sky and sea'. Among other works by Debussy with aquatic links are the piano preludes *La Cathédrale Engloutie* (The Submerged Cathedral) and *Ondine*.

Claude Debussy.

George Frederick Handel.

Debussy never did become a sailor, but if he had joined the French navy, he might well have found encouragement for his musical ambitions.

The French Marine de Guerre paid early attention to the training of its officers in dancing, music and the visual arts. From the seventeenth century a tradition was initiated that bore fruit in the establishment of Musiques de la Flotte (equivalent to the Royal Marine Band Service) and of Peintres de la Marine, official naval artists who are still appointed to the fleet for periods of between three to five years. Among those whose musical talents were encouraged over the last century or so were three composers of considerable talent: Roussel, Mariotte and Cras.

Albert Roussel (1869–1937), the most highly regarded of the three, served in the Marine from 1887–94, when he was invalided out. Roussel had shown great musical ability at an early age, but both his parents died when he was very young, and family circumstances steered him towards a career in the navy. He never lost his interest in music, and during a spell serving on a frigate in the Mediterranean he was able to try his hand at composition. He soon realised that music was his true calling and in due course was regarded as one of the leading French composers of his day. Notable successes were the ballet *Bacchus et Ariane* and the opera-ballet *Padmavati* on an Indian theme. Roussel chose to live on the Normandy coast and was buried in a cemetery overlooking the sea.[144]

Albert Roussel.

Antoine Mariotte (1875–1944) served in the Marine until 1897 when he resigned his commission to pursue a musical career. He is best known for his opera *Gargantua*, a burlesque of Rabelaisian character, and he was for a time administrator of the Opéra-Comique in Paris. A direct result of his seagoing experience was his orchestral *Esquisse Maritime* (Maritime Sketch).[145]

Jean Cras (1879–1932) remained in the French navy until he reached the rank of Rear-Admiral. He started composing at the age of thirteen, and later made sure his piano was embarked in ships he commanded. While he was captain of a destroyer in the Adriatic in the First World War he composed his opera *Polyphème* about the legendary one-eyed Sicilian giant Polyphemus, who was in love with the sea-nymph Galatea and was blinded by Ulysses. At the end of the opera, Lycas asks the now sightless Polyphemus, 'Where shall I lead you, good friend?' To which the giant replies, 'Towards the sea'. Another work by Jean Cras is a meditative nocturne called *Journal de Bord*, which depicts the hours from dusk to dawn while a ship sails on.[146]

British Composers and the Sea

The British Royal Navy appears to have produced no sailor composers of comparable talent. It was left to landlubbers to depict in sound the element which surrounds the British Isles and has played so large a part in our national destiny.

Edward Elgar.

The nineteenth century produced many major creators of music on the European mainland, but very few in these offshore islands until Edward Elgar (1857–1934) came along at the very end of the century with his *Enigma Variations*. Suddenly the continent realised that Britain had given birth to a composer to be reckoned with. Elgar's 'Pomp and Circumstance' marches allied him with military ceremonial, but he did create the poetic song cycle *Sea Pictures*, first performed at the Norwich Festival of 1899 by the statuesque Dame Clara Butt, dressed, according to Elgar, 'like a mermaid'.

At that time Sir Charles Villers Stanford (1852–1924) was firmly entrenched as Professor of Composition at the Royal College of Music, an

Benjamin Britten.

immensely influential teacher whose pupils included Frank Bridge (1879–1941) and Ralph Vaughan Williams (1972–58). There was tremendous patriotic enthusiasm in the first decade of the twentieth century for the navy and its building programme of Dreadnought battleships, and against that background Stanford's *Songs of the Sea* proved immensely popular as did his subsequent *Songs of the Fleet*. Both Vaughan Williams and Frank Bridge made substantial contributions to the repertoire of sea music: Vaughan Williams with his mighty 'Sea Symphony' for chorus and orchestra of 1909 and Bridge with his orchestral suite *The Sea* in 1910. Another Stanford pupil was John Ireland (1879–1962), who, in 1913, memorably set to music John Masefield's poem 'Sea Fever'. He also produced the piano suite *Sarnia*, which is largely inspired by the seas around the Channel Islands.

What was it about the early years of the twentieth century that prompt-ed so many British composers to produce fine music about the sea? In 1904 Frederick Delius (1862–1934) completed his *Sea Drift* for baritone solo, cho-rus and orchestra. It's a magical setting of words by Walt Whitman telling the story of two sea birds whose happy life together is destroyed by the death of the female. Arnold Bax (1883–1953) wrote two symphonic poems dominat-ed by thoughts of the sea – *Tintagel* and *The Garden of Fand*. Fand is a leg-endary Celtic heroine and her garden is the sea.

The sea played a major role in the life and works of the outstanding British musical genius of the next generation, Benjamin Britten (1913–76). He chose to live at Aldeburgh on the Suffolk coast, and that ancient town is the setting of his most famous and successful opera, *Peter Grimes*. The opera is based on a poem called 'The Borough', written in 1810 by George Crabbe. The central character, a fisherman, is an outsider who is driven to suicide by the suspicion and hostility of the Aldeburgh people. *Peter Grimes* was first performed at Sadlers Wells Theatre in London on 7 June 1945, a day that has been compared in its importance to British music with the premiere in June 1899 of Elgar's *Enigma Variations*. In 1951 Britten completed a second opera on a nautical theme – *Billy Budd*. The story by Hermann Melville leads to the execution of a virtuous young sailor for the accidental death of his tor-mentor, the master-at-arms, Claggart. Captain Vere respects Budd, but is unable to save him. 'In Billy Budd', wrote the music critic of *The Times*,

Ralph Vaughan Williams.

> … the protagonist is neither Vere nor Budd, but the sea. In the first act, the shrill wind, the salt tang and the eternal swell and surge of restless water envelop the listener, so that whatever happens aboard the 'Indomitable' he can never forget this relentless conditioning of sailors' lives.

The action of *Peter Grimes* is similarly dominated by the sea, and the four Sea Interludes that punctuate the action are among the opera's most telling passages.

Coda

It is clear that the sea has had a strong and inspirational influence on many composers. They have translated into the language of music the great rolling motion of the ocean's waves, the blue magnificence of sea and sky in fine weather, the glory of sunsets, the threatening power of storms and the sooth-ing, though sometimes disturbing, effects of a calm.

As for the seafarer, his hunger for music is just as great as that of any-one else. In the past he might have been an ill-educated professional who had to spend most of his energies in sailing his ship. Or he might have been a cultured passenger with an intellect well grounded in the arts. Both need-ed music in some form, the crude working song, the home-made concert, the more polished amateur or professional performance whether in peace-time or war conditions. On the rolling deck or in the heaving saloon, in the calm of a harbour or at the moment of departure, music at sea was, and remains, essential.

References

1 Music Takes to the Water

[1]See Hayes, William C, *The Scepter of Egypt, Part 1* (Harvard University Press 1953), p.269; Manniche, Lise, *Ancient Egyptian Musical Instruments* (Berlin 1975), p.45 and Fischer, H G, 'The Trumpet in Ancient Egypt', in *Pyramid Studies and Other Essays*, Egypt Exploration Society (London 1988), p.104.

[2]Morrison, J S and Coates, J F, *The Athenian Trireme* (Cambridge University Press 1986) and Manniche, Lisa, *Music and Musicians in Ancient Egypt* (London 1991), p.116.

[3]See Gelling, Peter and Davidson, Hilda Ellis, *The Chariot of the Sun* (London 1972), p.43 *et seq.*

[4]For good illustrations see Bildmappe No. 7 *Schiffe der Jäger und Bauern*, Evers, D and Ellmers, D, eds (Deutsches Schiffahrtsmuseum, Bremerhaven 1981).

[5]See Madsen, Jan Skamby and Crumlin-Pedersen, Ole, *To Skibsfund fra Falster* (Roskilde 1989). The Sutton Hoo Lyre reference: M and LA 193910–10203 (52) British Museum.

[6]See Perkins, R, *Rowing Chants and the Origins of Drottkvaedr Hattr*, Saga Book of Viking Club (London 1982–5), Vol.21, p.155 *et seq.* and Brade, Christine, 'Knöcherne Kernspaltflöten aus Haithabu' in *Berichte über die Ausgrabungen in Haithabu* (Neumünster 1978), p.24.

[7]See Salmen, Walther, *Der Fahrende Musiker im Europäischen Mittelalter* (Kassel 1960), p.95 *et seq.*

[8]Strohm, Reinhard, Music in Late Medieval Bruges (Oxford 1985), pp.77 and 114.

[9]See Field, C, *Old Times Afloat: a Naval Anthology* (London 1932), p.294. The miniature of St Louis has the reference no. MS fr 2829, fol 45v.

[10]See Villehardouin and Robert of Clari, chapter XIII, *To Bevetninger om Korsfarernes Erobung of Konstantinopel* (Danish Edition, Copenhagen 1931) and Wiel, Alethea, *The Navy of Venice* (London 1910), p.324.

[11]See Correia, A, *Alvoco das Várzeas* (Oliveira do Hospital Coimbra 1960).

[12]See O'Brien, Grace, *The Golden Age of German Music and Its Origins* (London 1953), p.42.

[13]The Russian pomor kotch project is directed by Alexander Skvortsov, Karelia Tamp, PB680, Petrozavopsk 185020 Russia.

[14]See Da la Roncière, Charles, *Histoire de la Marine Française* (Paris 1909) vol.1, p.372.

[15]See Firth, C H, ed., *Naval Songs and Ballads* (Navy Records Society, London 1908), p.2 *et seq.*

[16]The earliest surviving trumpets appear to be those excavated from the tomb of Tutankhamun who died *c.* 1350 BC. See Fischer, H G, 'The Trumpet in Ancient Egypt', in *Pyramid Studies and Other Essays*, Egypt

Exploration Society (London 1988).

[17]See Titcomb, Caldwell, unpublished dissertation, *The Kettledrums in Western Europe: Their History Outside the Orchestra* (Harvard University 1952).

[18]They had been first appointed on 18 May 1557. See De La Fontaine, *The Kings Musick* (London 1909).

[19]See Muñido, Francisco-Felipe Olesa, *La Organizacion Naval de los Estados Mediterraneos y en Especial de España Durante los Siglos XVI y XVII* (Madrid 1968), p.889.

2 Sounds of Supremacy at Sea

[20]See Correia, Gaspar, *Historia de India,* (Lisbon 1858) Livro 1, Capitolo III, p.14.

[21]*Ibid* p.15.

[22]See De Castanheda, Fernao Lopes, *Historia do Descrobimento e Conquista da India pelos Portugueses* (Coimbra 1551), Livro 1, Capitolo XCI, p.195.

[23]See Guillen Y Tato, Julio F, *La Carabela Santa Maria* (Madrid 1927), pp. 168–9 and Morison, E E, *Admiral of the Ocean Sea,* two vols (Boston 1942); also *Christopher Columbus Mariner* (New York 1942 and 1955), p.35 *et seq.*

[24]See Julien, Ch. A, Herval, R, and Beauchesne, Th., *Les Français en Amérique Pendant la Première Moitié du XVI Siècle,* Colonies et Empires, 2nd Series (Paris 1946).

[25]See Pulver, Jeffrey, *A Biographical Dictionary of Old English Music* (London 1927), p.117.

[26]*Ibid* p.124.

[27]See *Disquiciones Nauticas* (Madrid 1979), p.20.

[28]See de la Cal, Ramon Pevales, *Lepanto Sea Musica y Danza* (Museo Naval, Madrid 1972).

[29]At the departure of Stephen Burrough's ship *Serch Thrift* from Deptford in 1556, Sebastian Cabot, then aged eighty-four, gave alms to the poor and 'for the very joy he had to see the towardness of our intended discovery he entered into the dance himself among the rest of the young and lusty company'. Markham, A H, *Northward Ho* (London 1879), p.18.

[30]See Gosling, W G, *Life of Sir Humphrey Gilbert* (London 1911), p.225 *et seq.*; also Markham, A H, ed., *The Voyages and Works of John Davis,* Hakluyt Society (London 1880), pp.2–7.

[31]See Stephen, George A, *The Waits of the City of Norwich through Four Centuries* (Norwich 1933).

[32]See Pulver, Jeffrey, *A Biographical Dictionary of Old English Music* (London 1927), p.457.

[33]See De Crève Coeur, E Briand, *Peder Skram* (Copenhagen 1950), p.141.

[34]See De La Fontaine for this reference and those in previous paragraph.

[35]See Hansen, Thorkild, *Jens Munk* (Copenhagen 1965).

[36]See Islaendersen, Jon Olafssons, *Oplevelser som Bösseskytte under Christian IV* (Copenhagen 1905).

[37]See Merrien, Jean, *La Vie Quotidienne des Marins au temps du Roi Soleil* (Paris 1964), p.189 *et seq.*

[38]See Ogier, Charles, *Det Store Bilager i Kjöbenhavn 1634* (Copenhagen 1914), p.4.

[39]*Diary*, 23 April 1660. A new and fine edition was edited by Latham, R and Matthews, W (London 1970). Vol.X has a commentary on music at p.258.

[40]De La Fontaine.

[41]De La Fontaine.

[42]De La Fontaine.

[43]Boteler's *Dialogues* were published in transcription by the Navy Records Society (London 1929), vol.65, p.15 *et seq.*

3 Strike up the Band

[44]See Boxer, C R, *Fidalgos in the Far East 1550–1770* (The Hague 1948), p.79 *et seq.*

[45]I have not been able to gain access to an English edition of the official reports, but there are some useful notes by Cajsa Lund and David Kettlewell accompanying a compact disc, no. CAN CD005, made by Carizone of Klippinge Denmark. There is also a well-illustrated article by Anders Franzén in the American *National Geographic Magazine* for April 1989 (Washington).

[46]See Trendell, John, *A Life on the Ocean Wave* (Dover 1990), p6. This work gives a very thorough account of the history of Royal Marines bands.

[47]*Ibid* p.28.

[48]*Ibid* p.35.

[49]Forester, C S, *The Ship*, (London 1943), p.79.

[50]See Badcock, W S, (later Lovell, W S, Vice-Admiral), *A Personal Narrative of Events from 1799–1815* (Portsmouth *c.* 1840), p.45.

[51]National Maritime Museum Reference for Call; W88–18. See also articles in early volumes of *Mariner's Mirror*, especially Manwaring, G E, 'Lord Admiral's Whistle of Honour' (1923) vol.IX, p.75. Also De la Roncière, Charles, *Histoire de la Marine Française* (Paris 1909), vol.I, p.265. For the present-day use of the bosun's call see *Admiralty Manual of Seamanship* (HMSO 1979), vol.I, pp.367–371.

4 The Fiddler on the Maindeck

[52]Manuscript Riii. 19, Trinity College Library, Cambridge. Published Wright, T and Halliwell, J O, *Reliquae Antiquae* (London 1836) and Halliwell, J O, *Early Naval Ballads of England* (London 1841), Percy Society.

[53]See Müller-Blattau, Joseph, ed., *Deutsche Volkslieder* (Königstein im Taunus 1966), p.7.

[54]For the Venetian reference see: Kjersgaard, Erik, *Politikens Danmarks*

Historie (Copenhagen 1963), vol.IV, p.516. For the Yantlett reference see: Vogel, W, *Geschichte der Deutschen Seeschiffahrt*, (Berlin 1915), vol.1, p.110.

[55]See Chappell, William, *Old English Popular Music* (London 1893), p.21 and Walker, Ernest, *A History of Music in England* (Oxford 1970), p.7; also Müller-Blattau, Joseph, as in note 53 above (p.10).

[56]See Da la Roncière, Charles, *Histoire de la Marine Française* (Paris 1909), vol.I, p.268.

[57]See Godinho, Vitorino Magalhaes, *Documentos sobre a Expansao Portuguesa* (Lisbon, vol.11943, vol.21945 and vol.31956).

[58]See references at 19, also Madariaga, Salvador de, *Christopher Columbus* (London 1939), p.324.

[59]See Corbett, J S, *Drake and the Tudor Navy* (London 1898), pp.278–9.

[60]See Rodriguez-Salgado, M J, *Armada 1588–1988*, official catalogue of exhibition at the National Maritime Museum, Greenwich (London 1988), p.197; also Flanagan, Laurence and Stenuit, Robert, *Trésors de l'Armada* (Brussels 1986), p.184.

[61]National Maritime Museum, MS Ref. JOD 6. Published as *Diary of Rev. Henry Teonge* (London 1825), p.127.

[62]See Wilson, John, *Roger North on Music* (London 1959), p.41.

[63]See Witsen, N, *Aeloude en Hedendaegsche Scheeps-Bouw en Bestier* (Amsterdam 1671), pp.416–17. The engraving of the attack on Breda by Bartholomeus Dolendo is in the royal collections of H M The Queen of the Netherlands.

[64]See Dampier, William and Masefield, John, ed., *Dampiers Voyages* (London 1906), p.364 *et seq*.

[65]See Forrest, Thomas and Bassett, D K, *A Voyage to New Guinea 1774–6* (Kuala Lumpur: Oxford University Press 1969), pp.296–7.

[66]See Bellamy, R Reynell, *Ramblin Jack. The Journal of Captain John Cremer 1700–1774* (London 1936).

[67]See Journal of *Jomfru Susanne*. Manuscript in Ny Kgl Samling, Copenhagen Royal Library 2168.2°.

[68]MS in Middelburg Commercial Company Archives at Rijks Archief Middelburg, Ref. 165B. For other details of instruments owned by Netherlands naval officers and seamen, see Davids, C A, *Wat Lidt den Zeeman al verdriet Het Nederlandse Zeemanslied in de Zeiltied 1600–1900* (The Hague 1980).

[69]See MacDermott, *Life of Theobald Wolfe Tone* (London 1939), p.260.

[70]Osbeck, Pehr, *Dagbok Öfwer en Ostindisk Resa Aren 1750–52* (Stockholm 1757), p.313 *et seq*.

[71]Rask, Johannes; Nannestad F, ed., *En Kort og sandferdig Rejse-Beskrivelse til og fra Gvinea* (Trondheim 1754), p.16.

[72]Hammar, Hugo, *Fartygstyper i Swenska Ost Indiska Compagniets Flotta* (Gothenborg 1931), para 26.

[73]Chatterton, E K, *Ships and Ways of Other Days* (2nd edn, London 1924), p.265.

[74]Beaglehole, J C, *Journals of James Cook on his Voyages of Discovery*, vol.2. 'The Voyage of the *Resolution* and *Adventure*'; Hakluyt Society Extra Series

(CUP 1961), vol.xxxv, appendix, p.870.

[75]May, W E, National Maritime Museum: NMM9, B File letters: letter to Alick Rowe dated 23 November 1965.

[76]Beriot, Agnes, *Grands Voiliers autour du Monde* (Paris 1962), p.93.

[77]Ibid. p.169.

[78]See La Expedicion Malaspina (Madrid 1984), catalogue for exhibition. Especially De Persia, Jorge, 'La Documentacion de Expressiones Musicales en la Expedicion Malaspina' on p.cxxxi.

[79]Violin Ref. NMM.M57/28; Banjo Ref. NMM.59/9. See Scott, R F and Fuchs, V, *Scott's Last Expedition*, (Folio Society, London 1964 and 1965), p.74 *et seq*. There are other editions of his journals, of course. Also Doorly, Gerald S, *The Voyages of the Morning* (London 1916), p.33 *et seq*.

[80]See *Belgica, de Eerste Overwintering in Antarctica* (exhibition catalogue, National Scheepvaart-museum, Antwerp 1988), pp.22–3.

[81]Petersen, Carl, *Den Sidste Franklin Expedition med* Fox (Copenhagen 1860).

[82]NMM Ref. M52/43. For general reading see Langwill, Lyndesay G and Boston, Canon Noel, *Church and Chamber Barrel Organs* (2nd revised edn, Edinburgh 1970).

[83]Möhl, K E, *Breve fra Indien* (Copenhagen 1840), p.7.

[84]Gümoes, Frederik, 'Fra Sejlskibenes tid' *Dansk Havneblad*, March 1966. Danish National Maritime Museum, Kronborg.

[85]See Juel-Brockdorff, Niels, *Spredte Erindringer gennem 80 Aar* (Copenhagen 1960).

[86]See Holm, J, *Korvetten Heimdals Togt til de vestindiske Farvande i Aarene 1861–62* (Copenhagen 1863).

[87]See former periodical, *Vikingen* (Copenhagen 1972), no. 6, p.21 *et seq*.

[88]Svalgaard, Robert, *Krydstoldvaesenet, 1824–1904* (Esbjerg 1983), p.74.

[89]NMM. MS Ref: Henley Collection HNL33/9. His name was variously Christopher Martin/Marten/Mörtz. Eleven songs are included.

[90]*Ilione* journal is at NMM. MS Ref: JOD 158/2. For information regarding the journal in private hands, see the author.

[91]Notes to the gramophone records were published by Norske Hoechst A/S (Oslo 1969).

[92]MS in Danish National Maritime Museum, Kronborg. Lemmeke, Fritz, *En Tur paa Varmen* (1966).

[93]Christensen, C A, *Fyns Tidende*, 27 December 1961.

[94]Nielsen, H N M, *Saerdeles Haendelser Fra 1798–1816* (Copenhagen 1821).

[95]Johnson, Alvin Page, ed., *Under Sail and in Port in the* Glorious; *being the Journal from 1 May–30 October 1852 kept by Charlotte Page* (Salem 1950), entry for 5 July 1852.

[96]Runciman, Walter, *Before the Mast and After* (London 1924), p.146.

[97]Jewell, John H A, *American Neptune* (1951), vol.XI, p.189.

[98]Clausen, P H, *Erindringer fra mit Sömandsliv*, MS in Danish National Maritime Museum, Kronborg (1916).

[99]Schmidt, Fred., *Von den Bräuchen der Seeleute* (Hamburg 1947), p.68.

[100]Private communication from Dr Lauritz Pettersen, Director, Maritime Museum, Bergen, Norway.

[101]See Rayner, D A, *Escort. The Battle of the Atlantic* (London 1955), p.195.

[102]See Felix, John Henry, Nunes, Leslie and Senecal, Peter F, *The Ukulele. A Portuguese Gift to Hawaii* (Honolulu 1980).

[103]Sailmager, Laursen, *Horsens Avis*, journal, edn for 28 January 1956.

[104]Heims, P G, *Seespuk Aberglauben, Märchen und Schnurren* (Leipzig 1888).

[105]See *Illustreret Tidende* (Copenhagen 1880–1), xxi, p.167.

[106]See Danish National Maritime Museum *Yearbook* 1988, p.165.

[107]Spencer, Alfred, ed., *Memoirs of William Hickey*, 4 vols (London 1923–5), vol.1, p.197 *et seq.*

[108]MS at Maritime Institute of Ireland, Dublin. See article 'Trench's Travels' by Trench, C E F, in *Indian Ocean Review*, June 1988, p.3.

[109]MS 2168.2°, Ny Kgl Samling, Copenhagen Royal Library.

[110]See Hansen, C F, *Af mit Livs Historie*, 1824–1910. MS in Danish National Maritime Museum, Kronborg.

[111]MS in NMM Greenwich collections, Ref. JOD 171.

[112]MS in NMM Greenwich, Ref. P&O/91/8, F71.

[113]MS in NMM Greenwich, Ref. P&O/15/2, p.263.

[114]See Scholes, Percy A, ed., *Dr Burney's Musical Tours in Europe*, vol.2: *An 18th-Century Musical Tour in Central Europe and the Netherlands* (Oxford 1959), pp.70–1.

5 Shanties and Traditional Sea Songs

[115]There is an interesting report on this in the *Yorkshire Post* for 22 March 1988.

[116]Chapman, R W, ed., *Johnson's Journey to the Western Islands of Scotland and Boswell's Journal of a Tour to the Hebrides* (London 1924), p.56 and pp.264–5.

[117]Kennedy-Fraser, Marjory and Macleod, Kenneth, *Songs of the Hebrides* (London 1909); vol.1, p.xx *et seq.*

[118]*Ibid* xix.

[119]See Manniche, Lise, *Music and Musicians in Ancient Egypt* (London 1991), p.21.

[120]The origins of this rare publication remain rather obscure. It appears to have been published in Paris in 1549 and may have been written by Sir J I Wedderburn or Sir D Lindsay. There are later commentaries; one by J Leyden was published in Edinburgh in 1801.

[121]See Palmer, Roy, *Oxford Book of Sea Songs* (Oxford 1986), p.1.

[122]See Forrest, Thomas and Bassett, D K, *A Voyage to New Guinea 1774–1776* (Oxford University Press, Kuala Lumpar 1969), p.305.

[123]See Whall, W B, *Sea Songs and Shanties* (Glasgow 1920) pp.57 and 68. Captain Whall knew what the seaman sang, having started his collection of songs when he first went to sea in 1861.

[124]See Kendall Whaling Museum, Massachusetts, *Newsletter*, vol.6., no. 2, Summer 1988, p.2.

[125]See Bone, David W, *Capstan Bars* (Edinburgh 1931), p.110.

6 Soothing Airs

[126]Lee, J T, *Memoirs* (London 1836), p.9.

[127]See 'Mariner's Mirror', *Journal of Society for National Research* (1935), vol.21, no.4, p.450.

[128]See NMM 9. B files 1961–5: letter from Commander W E May to Alick Rowe dated 23 November 1965.

[129]See Hawkins, John H, *A General History of the Science and Practice of Music* (London 1776), p.222.

[130]See Mersenne, F M, *Questions Harmoniques* (Paris 1634), pp.100–2 and Agrippa, H C, *De Occulta philosophia, sive de magia libre tres* (Cologne 1533).

[131]Hawkins, J, *A General History of the Science and Practice of Music* (London 1776), vol.iv, pp.112–14.

[132]See Watt, James, 'Surgeons of the *Mary Rose*: The Practice of Surgery in Tudor England', in *Mariner's Mirror*, (1983), vol.69, p.3.

[133]See *Tidsskrift for Sövaesenet*, journal (Copenhagen 1937), p.233.

[134]See *Bulletin de l'Academie du Var*, 1987.

[135]See *Nautical Magazine* (London 1833), vol.II, p.285.

[136]See *Harmonicon* (London 1833), p.171.

[137]See Critchley, Macdonald and Henson, R A, *Music and the Brain* (London 1977), p.202, article by Harrer, G and Harrer, H, 'Music Emotion and Autonomic Function.'

[138]See Harrer, G and Harrer, H, *op. cit.*, p.204.

7 Music Born of the Sea

[139]See Deutsch, Carl Otto, *Handel, a Documentary Biography* (London 1955), p.77.

[140]See Deutsch, Otto Erich, *Admiral Nelson und Joseph Haydn* (Vienna 1982), p.105 *et seq.*

[141]See Jenkins, David and Visocchi, Mark, *Mendelssohn in Scotland* (London 1978), p.68 *et seq.*

[142]See Newman, Ernest, *Wagner Nights* (London 1949), p.15.

[143]See Lesure, Francois and Nichols, Roger, *Debussy Letters* (London 1987), p.141.

[144]See Sadie, Stanley, ed., *New Grove Dictionary of Music and Musicians* (London 1980), and Taillemite, Etienne, *Dictionnarie des Marins Français* (Paris 1982). Demuth, Norman, *Albert Roussel* (London 1947).

[145]See *New Grove Dictionary of Music and Musicians, op. cit.*

[146]See *New Grove Dictionary of Music and Musicians* and *Dictionnaire des Marins Français, op. cit.* Dumesnil, René, *La Musique en France entre les deux guerres 1919–1939* (Paris 1946).

Select Bibliography

In compiling this bibliography I have tried to avoid repeating titles given in the reference notes and to concentrate on works closely related to the theme of the book. There are many more works that might be included. For those interested I recommend application to the librarians at the National Maritime Museum, Greenwich, and the Royal College of Music, South Kensington, both of which have collections of manuscript as well as printed material. The Music Library at the British Library has outstandingly important collections and a very good Reading Room Service.

In the case of De la Fontaine, *The Kings Music* (1909), Dr Andrew Ashbee has published a comprehensive revised edition under the title *Records of English Court Music, 1485–1714,* of which vol. III appeared in 1988. I have used references from the earlier version, but the Ashbee edition should also be studied.

For the official records of Royal Marines and Royal Naval Bands or their equivalents overseas, recourse must be had to the National Archives or to the relevant Archives Nationales. I am very grateful to Dr Henning Henningsen for his help with this and the reference notes.

1 Music

Abraham, Gerald	*Rimsky-Korsakov*	London 1945
van Acht, R J M	*Volksmuziek en Volks-instrumenten in Europa*	Haags Gemeente Museum 1983
Bacharach, A L	*The Musical Companion*	London 1947
Baldwin, David	*The Chapel Royal*	London 1990
Bantock, Granville	*One Hundred Folk Songs of all Nations*	Boston, USA 1911
Baring-Gould, S, Sheppard, H F and Bussell, F W	*Songs of the West*	London 1913
Cooke, Deryck	*The Language of Music*	Oxford 1959 and 1962
Creighton, Helen	*Maritime Folk Songs*	London 1979
Davies, J Glyn	*Cerddi Portinllaen*	Liverpool 1954
Davies, J Glyn	*Cerddi Huw Puw*	1954
Davies, Walford	*The Pursuit of Music*	London 1936

Dent, Edward J	*Opera*	Penguin 1951
Deutsch, Otto Erich	*Admiral Nelson und Joseph Haydn*	Vienna 1982
Doerflinger, William Main	*Shantymen and Shantyboys Songs of the Sailor and Lumbermen*	New York 1951
Einstein, Alfred	*Music in the Romantic Era*	New York 1947
Elders, Willem	*Composers of the Low Countries*	Oxford 1991
Elkin, Robert	*Old Concert Rooms of London*	London 1955
Farinelli, Carlos Broschi and Borrero, Consolación Morales	*Fiesta Reales en el Reinadde Fernando V1*	Madrid 1987
Fellowes, Edmund H	*William Byrd*	Oxford 1923
Firth, C H, ed.	*Naval Songs and Ballads*	Navy Records Society, London 1908
Geiringer, Karl	*Instruments in the History of Western Music*	London 1978
Harlow, Frederick Pease	*American Chanteys*	Barre, Barre Bazette 1962
Hottois, Isabelle	*L'Iconographie Musicale la Bibliothèque Royale, Albert I*	Brussels 1982
Hugill, Stan	*Songs of the Sea*	McGraw Hill, Maidenhead 1977
Karolyi, Otto	*Introducing Music*	Penguin 1981
Kendall, Alan	*Music its Story in the West*	London 1980
Kennedy-Fraser, Marjorie and Macleod, Kenneth	*Songs of the Hebrides,*	London 1909 and 1917 two vols
Lesure, François and Nicols, Roger	*Debussy Letters*	London 1987
Lippman, Edward A	*Musical Thought in Ancient Greece*	London 1964
Mackerness, E D	*A Social History of English Music*	London 1964
Muller-Blattau, Joseph	*Deutsche Volkslieder*	Königstein im Taunus 1966
Myers, Bernard S	*Art and Civilization*	London 1967
Newman, Ernest	*Wagner Nights*	London 1974

Nagel, W	'Aanalen der Englischen Hofmusik', supplement to vol. 26 of *Monatshefte für Musik geschichte*	Breitkopf & Härtel 1896
O'Brien, Grace	*The Golden Age of German Music and its Origins*	London 1953
Olleson, Edward, ed.	*Modern Musical Scholarship*	London 1978
Palmer, Roy, ed.	*Oxford Book of Sea Songs*	OUP 1986
Raynor, Henry	*A Social History of Music*	London 1972
Reese, Gustave	*Music in the Middle Ages*	London 1941
Reese, Gustave	*Music in the Renaissance*	New York 1959
Rimsky-Korsakov, N A	*My Musical Life*	London 1974
Robertson, Alec and Stevens, Denis	*Pelican History of Music*, vol. 1, 1960; vol. 2, 1984; 3, 1986	Penguin, Harmondsworth
de Roda, Cecilio	*La Musica Profana en el Reinado de Carlos I*	Bilbao, 1912
Scholes, Percy A	*The Mirror of Music* two vols.	London and OUP 1947
Scholes, Percy A	*The Oxford Companion to Music*, revised edn	OUP 1960
Scholes, Percy A	*The Concise Oxford Dictionary of Music 2nd edn*	OUP 1977
Simpson, C M	*The British Broadside Ballad and its Music*	New Brunswick 1966
Smith, L A	*Music of the Waters*	London 1888
Stevens, John	*Music and Poetry in the Early Tudor Court*	London 1961
Szabolcsi, Benee	*A History of Melody*	London 1965
Torr, Edward	*The Trumpet*	London 1988
Trendell, John	*Operation Music Maker*	Eastney 1982
Trendell, John	*A Life on the Ocean Wave*	Deal 1990
Trendell, John	*Colonel Bogey to the Fore*	Deal 1992
Walker, Ernest	*A History of Music in England*	OUP 1970
von Westernhagen, Curt	*Wagner*	Cambridge 1981
Whall, W B	*Sea Songs and Shanties*, 4th edn	Glasgow 1920
Woodfill, Walter	*Musicians in English Society*	Princeton, USA 1953
Yvart, Jacques	*Florilège de la Chanson de Mer*	Paris 1980

2 Maritime

Bellec, François	*La généreuse et tragique expédition La Pérouse*	Rennes 1985
Bellec, François	*Océans des Hommes*	Paris 1987
van Beylen, Jules	*Zeilvaart Lexicon*	Weesp 1985
Cornuault, J	*Les Forceurs du Passage du Nord-Ouest*	Paris 1971
Davis, Ralph	*The Rise of the English Shipping Industry in the 17th and 18th Centuries*	London 1962; NMM 1972
Debenham, Frank	*Discovery and Exploration*	London 1960
Forster, Honore	*The South Sea Whaler*	Kendall, Mass. 1985
Greenhill, Basil	*Sailing for a Living*	London 1962
Lewis, Michael	*A Social History of the Navy*	London 1960
Lloyd, Christopher	*The British Seaman*	London 1968 and 1970
Lord, Walter	*A Night to Remember*	London 1956 and 1958
Lord, Walter	*The Night Lives On*	London 1986
Marsden, Peter	*The Wreck of the Amsterdam*	London, 1974 and 1985
Morrison, Samuel Eliot	*Christopher Columbus Mariner*	New York 1955
National Scheepvaart museum Antwerp, catalogue	*Belgica; de eerste Overwintering in Antarctica 1897–1899*	Antwerp 1988
Ormond, Richard and others	*Mutiny on the Bounty*	London, NMM and Manorial Research 1989
Penrose, Boies	*Travel and Discovery in the Renaissance*	Harvard 1960
de Raeve, Jacques and Durosquel Jean-Marie	*Trésors de l'Armada*	Brussels 1986
Robinson, Charles N	*The British Tar in Fact and Fiction*	London 1909
Rodriguez-Salgado, M J	*Armada 1588–1988*	National Maritime Museum, London and Penguin Books, Harmondsworth 1988
Rudolph, Wolfgang	*Maritime Kultur der Südlichen Ostsee Küste*	Rostock 1983

Scammell, G V	*The World Encompassed: The first European maritime empires c. 800–1650*	London 1981
Scammell, G V	*The English Chartered Trading Companies and the Sea*	National Maritime Museum, London 1980
Scott, R F	*Scott's Last Expedition*	Folio Society, London 1964
Stammers, M	*The Passage Makers*	Brighton 1978
Sutton, Jean	*Lords of the East*	London 1981
Villain-Gandossi, C	*Le Navire Médiéval à travers les Miniatures*	CNRS Paris 1985
Villanueva, Carlos	*El Portico de la Gloria*	Santiago de Compostela 1988
Waters, D W	The English Pilot: English Sailing Directions and Charts and the Rise of English Shipping'	*Journal of Royal Institute of Navigation*, vol. 42, No. 3, 1989
Weibust, Knut	*Deep Sea Sailors*	Stockholm, Nordiska Museum, English edn 1976

Picture Credits

Index

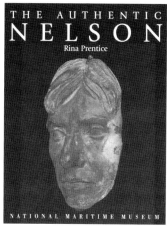

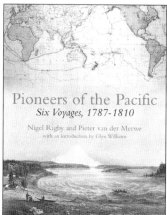
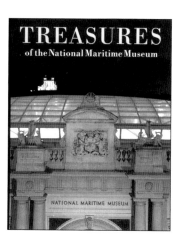

National Maritime Museum Publishing

At NMMP we bring you beautifully illustrated, thoroughly-researched and competitively priced books that explore all aspects of the sea, ships, time and the stars.
To find out more visit us at **www.nmm.ac.uk/publishing**

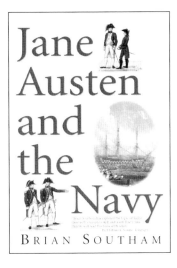

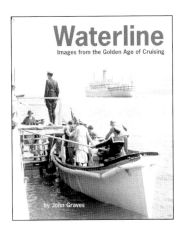

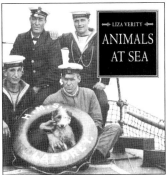

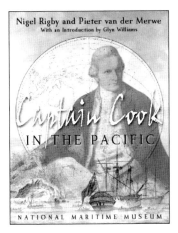

National Maritime Museum Products

If you would like to order any of these books, or to view our unique range of National Maritime Museum products please call 020 8312 6700 or visit **www.nmm.ac.uk/shop**